Close Encounters With The Fourth Estate

Close Encounters With The Fourth Estate

A SERIES OF TRUE LIFE SHORT STORIES

By Journalists

Thomas J. Morrow, Sam Lowe, Cecil F. Scaglione and John Beatty

© 2017 Thomas J. Morrow, Sam Lowe, Cecil F. Scaglione and John Beatty

All rights reserved.

ISBN-13: 9781973939542
ISBN-10: 1973939541

This book is dedicated to our wives, our families, friends and former colleagues

Part I: Ah, The Life of a Writer

By
Sam Lowe

"I come from Kensal, North Dakota, where the only thing stopping that cold Canadian wind was a single strand of barbed wire fence out north of town."

Thomas J. Morrow, Sam Lowe, Cecil F. Scaglione and John Beatty

Editor's Note: *Sam Lowe is reporter, editor, feature writer and long-time daily newspaper columnist. A native of North Dakota, Sam worked as sports reporter, editor in Jamestown, N.D., later moving to Arizona and the Scottsdale Daily Progress and on to the Phoenix Gazette where he was a columnist. For the past several years, Sam has worked as a feature writer, as well a publishing 14 books, primarily on Arizona subjects.*

William "Captain Kirk" Shatner, left, and "Star Trek" creator Gene Roddenberry, right, came to Arizona. For me, it was a long-anticipated interview. It was an experience where I had not gone before.

My Day as a Trekkie

PHOENIX, ARIZONA – WHILE GOING through the learning process required to become a reporter, then a columnist, I discovered that often, long-anticipated interviews would be exactly what I hoped they'd be. But sometimes, they turned out to be major disappointments. My dealings with the creator and crew of "Star Trek" were classic examples of both.

On the plus side, Gene Roddenberry and Persis Khambatta were absolute delights. But William Shatner and Susan Oliver...well...not so much.

Remembering them in chronological order:

When offered the chance to meet and write about Persis Khambatta, I made no effort to conceal my eagerness. Nobody else in *The Phoenix Gazette* newsroom had any idea who she was, but I knew. She was not only a former Miss India (she won the title at age 15), but she was also Lt. Ilia, a Deltan navigator aboard the USS Enterprise in "Star Trek: The Motion Picture." (I am obligated to interject here that the fact that she was gorgeous had nothing to do with my willingness to conduct the interview. Admittedly, it may have sparked my interest somewhat, but my main focus was on her connection to "Star Trek." Really. I wouldn't lie about anything that important.)

So we met and I immediately noticed that she had very dark hair. While it's not unusual for an actress to have very dark hair, the woman she portrayed in the movie was bald. Not that there's anything wrong with that. It's just how things were on the planet Delta. Obviously, since the movie had been released several months prior and I had already seen it twice, her hair had grown back. She said she didn't mind being bald but the makeup people had to shave her head every day to keep it nice and shiny because she refused to wear a rubber bald piece. Then she added that she had given up sex during the filming of the movie. It just came out of the blue. I most certainly didn't ask her about it. She explained that it had something to do with the purity of the role.

She was nice and she was pretty. Unfortunately, her role in the movie didn't result in a stellar film career in the United States so she returned to India to work in television. She died of a heart attack in 1998. She was only 47.

But Lieutenant Ilia lives on, still boldly going into space, the final frontier.

A year later, a friend involved in movie production called and asked if I'd be an extra in a sci-fi film being shot in Cordes Junction north of Phoenix. I quickly agreed when he said William Shatner was starring and would agree to an interview. As a "Star Trek" fan from the first episode, being offered a chance to discuss outer space with Capt. James T. Kirk was like an invitation to Nirvana.

So we met behind one of the cameras but then came the bad news: Before I even got my first question posed, he told me not to ask him anything about "Star Trek." Nothing. No trivia. No behind-the-scenes incidents. No bloopers. No nothing. Instead, he wanted to concentrate on his current project, a movie entitled "Kingdom of the Spiders." Disappointed but devious, I tried to sneak in some Trekkie lore in my questions, asking things like, "Remember that episode where you and Spock had to fight giant spiders?" He didn't even acknowledge the query. He was adamant. Not only adamant, but unswerving to the point of being downright brusque.

He did, however, answer every other query I put to him, and he graciously posed for a photo, so it wasn't a total loss. I went to see the movie when it came to Phoenix. It wasn't very good. It's about giant tarantulas taking over a town. In the final scene, Shatner and his female companion are encased in a huge web and were about to meet their doom by becoming an arachnid snack. He should have stuck with "Star Trek." Things like that never happened when he commanded the USS Enterprise.

Susan Oliver was in just one "Star Trek" episode, but it was memorable. She portrayed Vina, a horribly disfigured woman who, through powerful hypnosis administered by some aliens, became a suitable (but green-skinned) mate for Jeffrey Hunter in the pilot production of the series. The pilot was eventually chopped into two parts and incorporated into the regular schedule. In it, Hunter's character was badly damaged in a space accident and the crew of the USS Enterprise returned him to a planet where the inhabitants used hypnosis to make things seem different that what they really were. So he was hypnotized to good health and fell in love with the already-hypnotized Vina and, we were left to assume, they lived happily ever after.

The plot was a bit confusing, but Susan Oliver was hot. Green, but hot. She was also gorgeous, alluring, inviting, and tempting. It was lust at first sight for me. Imagine, then, my excitement upon hearing that she was going to appear at a book-signing event in Litchfield Park, a Phoenix suburb and, as the paper's official "Star Trek" expert, I was assigned to cover it. Perhaps we could...you know...hit it off. It could happen. So I motored to the book store, entered the room and there she was. Susan Oliver. And she was hot. She was also gorgeous, alluring, tempting and several other adjectives that most definitely would not appear in my report. I took a chair close to her and waited while others asked inane questions about her book. Then, when it came my turn, I put it to her directly: "Do you remember when you were Vina?"

She gave me a blank stare, which quickly morphed into a glare, then to a look of absolute disdain. "Who?" she replied and she wasn't smiling. I knew then that my hopes for a romantic liaison were dissolving faster than the Romulans did when they got phasered. "Vina," I responded but it was weak and wimpy and she didn't even bother to answer.

She turned to answer more questions about her book. I rose with as much dignity as I had left and headed for the exit. Susan Oliver, my

Vina, my true lust, smiled an insincere smile and said, "Oh, must you leave so soon? Well, stay in touch."

Even a broken-hearted Trekkie could recognize sarcasm.

Disturbing thoughts cascaded through my mental facilities as I prepared to meet Gene Roddenberry, the brilliant mind behind "Star Trek" and thus the object of my deepest admiration. I wanted him to be a nice person because I had been a Trekkie since before the the word had been invented. But I had heard that he was a difficult interview and that he could get feisty with reporters who asked tough questions. As a "Star Trek" groupie since the first episode, I most certainly wasn't going to ask any tough questions because if there was anybody I didn't want mad at me, it was Gene Roddenberry.

So we met and in the first nano-second, I knew all was well. He was congenial, affable, serious but not the least bit confrontational. And, most important of all, he wanted to talk about his new series, "Star Trek: The Next Generation," and expressed some concern that the media might gun it down before it aired. So he was trying hard to avoid any negative publicity. We spent about an hour together and Roddenberry answered every one of my questions, even though some of them were downright dumb. Like when I asked if William Shatner, during his portrayal of Capt. Kirk, wore a hair piece ("I never asked him"). Or if Nichelle Nichols, who played Lt. Uhura, was a sexy as she appeared on television ("Yes, most definitely yes").

It was, up until later when I became single, one of the best hours I ever spent with any human being. Then it got even better when Roddenberry gave me a Star Fleet communications device and made me an honorary member of the USS Enterprise crew.

And since that day, I have lived long and prospered.

Persis Khambatta was not only a former Miss India (she won the title at age 15), but she was also Lt. Ilia, a Deltan navigator aboard the USS Enterprise in "Star Trek: The Motion Picture."

A Few Moments with Silver's Owner

**The Lone Ranger, a.k.a. Clayton Moore,
stopped by to visit with one of his oldest fans.**

FOUNTAIN HILLS, ARIZONA – WHEN I was a lad, the thirty minutes between 4:30 and 5 on Monday, Wednesday and Friday afternoons were sacred. During that most-holiest of holy times, like all our faithful companions across the country, my brothers and I gathered in front of the old wood-boxed radio that was the featured attraction of our family's living room and turned the dial to 540, WDAY in Fargo. Then we waited. Soon, the magic words spread across the living room, those magic words that included the classic phrase, "... return with us to those thrilling days of yesteryear, when from out of the past come the thundering hoofbeats of the great horse Silver ..."

And then the Lone Ranger galloped into our living room. Always on time, always ready to save us from the variety of bad persons who inhabited the air waves in that glorious era. Equally important, he never asked us for monetary contributions to help in his ongoing battle against evil. Captain Midnight wanted us to send in our allowances to purchase his secret decoder badge; Sergeant Preston offered us uranium tracing rings in exchange for a quarter. But the Lone Ranger merely requested that we, in so many words, behave ourselves and be nice to others.

But times changed. He moved on to television, then the movies, always portrayed by Clayton Moore. And I, now much too sophisticated to return to those thrilling days of yesteryear, went to college, got a job, and took up space in the real world.

And even though he was still sort of my personal hero, Moore got ambushed by time and was forced out of his role as the Lone Ranger in the movies and on TV. He still made public appearances as the masked man at a variety of events, from film conventions to gatherings for young people who needed instruction on how to be honest, truthful and just plain old good. Then, in 1981, he got bushwhacked.

That year, Hollywood announced plans for a new movie about the Lone Ranger but Clayton Moore wasn't going to portray him. Instead, the producers boldly announced that they had selected Klinton Spilsbury, who had never portrayed anyone in any entertainment medium. That wasn't the worst part, however. To make certain the public didn't confuse the real Lone Ranger (Clayton Moore) with their sophomoric version (Klinton Spilsbury, who didn't even know how to spell his first name correctly), the movie makers got an injunction against Moore, forbidding him to wear the mask that identified him as the true guardian of justice in the Old West.

It was under those circumstances that I met my childhood hero at a youth rally in Fountain Hills. Considering that he was well over 60 years of age at the time, he was in remarkable shape and even though he was forced to replace his mask with a pair of dark sunglasses, there was no doubt that he was the Lone Ranger. The real one. Not some imposter who flunked out of spelling class. But the lack of a mask couldn't diminish the power of that voice that had represented goodness, truth, justice and the American way three times a week those many years before. That voice which echoed across the Old West with honor and dignity. That voice which should be framed and hung on a wall in the Smithsonian Institute.

We talked about the earlier days, when there was some kind of good left in the world because of him, and he expressed disappointment about the attempt to obscure his persona. But his speech to the young people was upbeat without any mention of the new movie and the injustice that had befallen him.

A while later, although I felt like a traitor in doing so, I paid six bucks to watch "The Legend of the Lone Ranger" when it reached the local movie houses. It was a wasted evening. The movie stunk. The plot stunk. Most of the writing stunk. And Klinton Spilsbury was worse at acting than he was at spelling.

In a way, I felt there was some justice in that.

An Afternoon with Joe

SCOTTSDALE, ARIZONA – HERE'S A question that doesn't get asked very often: What do Sam Lowe and baseball Hall of Famers Stan Musial, Red Schoendienst and Enos Slaughter all have in common? The answer: Each one was, at one time or another, a teammate of Joe Garagiola.

Naturally, there's an illogical explanation for the association but, in a sense, there'ome truth involved. I shall attempt to explain.

Garagiola played major league baseball for nine years, most of the time with the St. Louis Cardinals, but also with the Chicago Cubs, Pittsburgh Pirates and New York Giants. (He once declared that he because he played for so many teams, he was little more than "a model for major league baseball uniforms.") In 1946, his rookie year, he went 6-for-19 in the World Series to help the Cardinals defeat the Boston Red Sox. Musial, Schoendienst and Slaughter were also members of that team.

After retirement from baseball, Garagiola turned to radio and television. He cohosted "The Today Show," often sat in for Johnny Carson on "The Tonight Show," emceed the Westminster Kennel Club's annual awards show, and announced baseball games for a variety of radio networks. He also received a multitude of major baseball honors, including election into to the Hall of Fame as a broadcaster.

He was still announcing Arizona Diamondback games when I was called upon, as part of my duties as a columnist for *The Phoenix Gazette*, to leave my office and present my body to the public by participating in an athletic competition with the Phoenix Stars.

(The Stars were an assortment of media personalities who were skilled at using hair spray, posing, and inflating their own egos, but with extremely limited athletic abilities. So limited, in fact, that we never won a game during our six-year existence. We got beat in tag football, basketball, softball, baseball, tiddly-winks, tricycle racing, tennis and doggie-dressing.)

On this particular day, we were scheduled to play softball against a team composed of former Chicago Cubs. Due to our poor won-lost record (0-everything), we occasionally attempted to rectify the situation by bringing in a ringer. Garagiola was no longer a television star so he couldn't hurt his image by playing for us, so he agreed to join our team for this one game. It was a noble idea that had never worked before but, in this situation we figured his mere presence might inspire us to at last reach the pinnacle of victory.

And so, we took the field as the home team.

The first five ex-Cubs hit home runs. The sixth batter only doubled, and we took that as an indication that they were weakening and we might have a chance. Then the next four batters homered and we were behind 10-0 in the top of the first inning with nobody out. Mercifully, the game officials had installed a rule that declared a team could only bat around twice in one inning so we escaped by giving up a mere 18 runs.

When we came to bat in the bottom of the first, Garagiola was our lead-off hitter and he lofted a fly ball to left field, where former Cub Billy Williams, another Hall of Fame member, graciously let it plop in front of him. So, we had a man on with nobody out. Although not enough to scare the Cubs, it might indicate a rally. But I followed with sharply-hit six-hopper back to the pitcher that led to a double play and there were two outs. We never got another baserunner. Following the example they set in the first inning, the Cubs scored another 18 runs in both the second and third. At that point, everyone involved decided that sitting in a saloon would be a lot more fun than watching old guys run around the bases, so the game was called at the end of three.

Garagiola was gracious in defeat. In his post-game analysis, he said he thought we might have held the score down if we had forfeited the game rather than show up at all.

The Day Life Flashed Before Me

A classic pose I captured with a cumbersome Speed Graphic camera during a campaign stop by soon-to-be one of our iconic Presidents – John F. Kennedy.

JAMESTOWN, NORTH DAKOTA – DURING his short lifetime, John F. Kennedy faced many photographers burdened with Speed Graphic cameras. But until he encountered mine, he had never been attacked by one.

As sports editor of *The Jamestown Sun*, I had very little interest in politics. My reporting duties centered around 78-yard touchdown runs, last-second baskets, gargantuan home runs and how to sneak a flask of peppermint schnapps past the stadium guards. In addition to describing such feats in prose, I was also the staff photographer, assigned to capture everyone and everything from politicians to prize heifers to blizzards and beauty queens on film. With a Speed Graphic camera.

Under those circumstances, John F. Kennedy and I had a rather ignominious encounter.

Kennedy was campaigning to become the Democratic candidate for president and apparently thought North Dakota's votes were crucial to the effort. So crucial, in fact, that he showed up in February, more than four months before the annual Stutsman County Fair, the normal forum for public office seekers.

And the Speed Graphic and I were assigned to document the event.

Speed Graphics were wonderful cameras, but they were cumbersome and required large amounts of preparation. The film was not in rolls, but in 4-by-5-inch sheets that had to be loaded into individual holders. Each holder held only two sheets of film, so every photo assignment required a predetermined number of holders, depending upon the importance of the subject matter. The mayor and the winner of the Kiwanis scholarship were worth one holder. So were prize-winning cattle at the county fair; Miss Jamestown and the North Dakota Dairy Princess got two.

The camera also required flash bulbs. They were about the size of a 25-watt light bulb or a medium-sized onion and were mounted into a flash gun attached to the side of the camera prior to taking a photo. We always stuffed at least a dozen bulbs into the camera case, which resembled a small steamer trunk or a plumber's tool kit. By the time the film was loaded, the camera inserted, the flash gun and bulbs sequestered, and all the other vitals stuffed into the case, the weight exceeded 25 pounds. Veteran photographers of those days were particularly susceptible to hernia.

Then, once the subject had been located and ordered to hold that smile, the camera required a series of complicated maneuvers:

Un-snap case. Remove camera. Attach flash gun. Open front of camera. Pull bellows out. Lock it onto track. Remove lens cap. Insert film holder into back of camera. Remove slide from holder so film could be exposed. Screw flash bulb in. Cock shutter. Aim. Focus. Push the button.

Missing just one step meant no photo, or at least a retake. Decidedly more aware of all the requirements due to the importance of the situation, my Speed Graphic and I set out to take a picture of John F. Kennedy. I arrived early to secure a good spot and waited. Soon, a mini-parade led by the mayor, two councilmen, Miss Jamestown and four Democratic candidates for the state legislature marched Kennedy up to the second floor of the Elks Club, now brightly festooned with red, white and blue banners and card tables loaded down with neatly sliced carrots, peeled radishes, coffee urns and deviled eggs.

One by one, the mayor, councilmen, office-seekers and Miss Jamestown delivered well-prepared orations of welcome. Kennedy gracefully acknowledged the honors they accorded him with smiles and nods, then rose to give his address, while I nervously began the litany of camera preparation.

Kennedy was New England gracious and boyishly charming but nobody actually paid much attention to his speech because it was his presence that mattered, not what he said. Besides, he pretty well had the nomination locked up so his words drifted off into the vast nothingness where political speeches go to die.

I waited patiently until the talking was over, then approached Kennedy and asked if he'd pose for a photo. He looked at my Speed Graphic and said, with a New England chuckle, "That's a pretty big camera to use on a politician." But he smiled and turned slightly away from the camera, obviously aware that if he looked directly at me, he'd take a 250-watt direct hit from the flash.

With slightly trembling hands, I aimed, focused and pushed the button to ignite the bulb.

For a split second, nothing happened. Kennedy was posing, I was aiming but there was no sudden burst of light.

Then, in the next split second, everything happened.

Instead of lighting up the room the way it was supposed to, the bulb just went "pop," then ejected itself from the flash gun, making a kind of "feeezle feeezle feeezle" noise while heading toward the man who wanted to be president.

In the next split second, I was surrounded by two big guys wearing dark suits. One of them yanked the Speed Graphic from my hands while a third big guy clad in similar attire jumped in front of Kennedy. Then when the errant missile plopped about four feet short of its apparent target, he ended its miserable existence with a well-placed stomp. It all happened so fast there wasn't even time for an image of life as a federal prisoner to formulate inside my befuddled brain.

Fortunately for me and my Speed Graphic, and because fizzling flash bulbs don't achieve much distance, Kennedy did not appear the least bit upset. Instead, he reacted with a smile and said, "Did the Republicans send you?"

Once assured that his boss was safe, one of the big guys did a cursory examination of my Speed Graphic, then returned it to me and solemnly warned, "Don't do that anymore." Now shaken more than any other time in my life, I inserted another bulb while Kennedy took up a new pose. I pushed the button, the flash went off, Kennedy was safe and I wasn't about to ask him to hold still for another attempt. Then I rushed back to the office, went into the darkroom, placed the single sheet of film into the developing chemicals and prayed.

For the entire five minutes required for processing that one negative, I was making promises that if the photo turned out all right, I'd quit swearing at the Speed Graphic and take better care of my flash bulbs.

The pleas worked. The photo was a little grainy but it was good enough to run on the front page. Two days later, the editor received a letter from a Kennedy aide, thanking him for covering the appearance in a kindly manner. The editor showed the letter to me, but kept it for his own files.

I voted for Kennedy that November. It seemed like the decent thing to do.

My Time With "The Greatest" Cassius Clay, a.k.a. Muhammad Ali

Muhammad Ali sitting on a train passing through Jamestown, North Dakota

JAMESTOWN, NORTH DAKOTA – CLARICE Klein, the receptionist, buzzed my desk and I let her repeat the message twice before responding because her voice over the intercom had the quality of whipped cream – silky, smooth, and never quite enough. "Your father's on the phone," she purred. Then, as if to allay any suspicion that I might consider her snoopy, she added, "At least, it sounds like him." She offered no explanation of why she knew my father's voice on the telephone, and I didn't care. As long as she told me with that vocal display of sensuality.

Pushing aside the recurring daydream I normally associated with Clarice and her ability to get my full attention merely by whispering into the intercom, I picked up the phone. It was my dad, calling long distance from Fargo. He began with an apology because it was a collect call, but quickly noted that my employer could afford it, then justified that supposition with a brief analysis of a newspaper publisher's income versus that of a railroad man forced to walk miles in the cold of winter checking flatbeds and cattle cars for hot boxes. Seconds later, I became aware that he had something more important to convey because he discontinued his usual account of life and all its unfairnesses before getting to the part about how every step he took was uphill in three feet of snow and he had to lug a fourvolt lantern from one end of a 135-car freight train to the other while wearing itchy woolen underwear, the defense he always used when any of his children asked for a raise in allowance.

So, his version of why the world lacked equality was superseded by the real reason for his call, and his voice took on an edge of mystery as he confided, "Cassius Clay is on the three-seventeen passenger train." He said it in a tone unusual for him because he was, most of all, a hard-working railroad man who rarely got excited unless the Minnesota Twins were playing in the World Series, an occurrence so rare that only defeating his wife in cribbage came close to equaling it.

"It'll be pulling into town in about a half-hour," he added. "Just thought the editor of the Jamestown Sun should know about it." He made no effort to conceal his pride at being the father of the editor of the paper. Then, rather than burden the accounting department with further expense, he ended the call with, "It's up to you now, my boy. You're the editor."

I hung up and gave some momentary consideration of disrupting the newsroom with juvenile shouts and exclamations similar to "I know something you don't!" The revelation that Cassius Clay was going to be in Jamestown was front page news. To my knowledge, nobody that famous had ever stopped at the local station before. Unless Wallace Beery counted and those who reported his presence weren't certain it was him because they had only seen him, or somebody that looked like him, looking out the window of the dining car as the train was pulling out of town.

But there wasn't time for jubilation. The wall clock said it was 2:34 in the afternoon so the 3:17 was already passing through Valley City, only about 40 minutes away. It would take ten minutes to walk from the office to the depot, probably another five minutes to locate Cassius Clay because my dad didn't know for sure which car he was riding in, and, despite the fact that this was front page news, the train was only going to stop in Jamestown for twelve minutes.

Although I attempted to conceal my inner excitement over the prospect of meeting the heavyweight boxing champion of the world, Wayne Deery, one of our advertising representatives and also the son of a railroad man, observed that I was not acting in my usual calm demeanor and asked why. I gave him a brief, but informative, answer and asked if he'd like to come along, assuming that two of us would have a better chance of finding which car carried the champ. He readily agreed.

The four of us – the 3:17, Wayne, me and Cassius Clay – arrived at the station almost simultaneously. We boarded and implemented our hastily-organized strategy: Wayne goes right, I go left, both running down the narrow aisles yelling, "Cassius Clay! Cassius Clay! Are you in here?"

(This may not have been a proper salutation for a world champion but we had less than twelve minutes to, as they used to say back in those glorious times when newspapers actually printed news that hadn't been already spewed to a mindless public by television and computers, get the scoop.)

There were four passenger cars. Wayne, younger and thus more excitable than I, got through his pair with no positive results so he came dashing back toward me as I was calling for Cassius in my third coach. My task took longer because the passengers in my assigned section were seated in private compartments so I had to pound on some doors. Nobody answered, not even when I identified myself as a reporter for the local newspaper. Not even when I said it would be an honor to interview him. Not even when I said Sonny Liston was a bum with as much sincerity as I could muster, considering that I had never met Sonny Liston. And the train would be pulling away from the station in less than eight minutes.

Finally, in one of those acts of desperation that were constant companions of small town reporters, I remembered that shortly after he had defeated Liston to become the champion, Clay had joined the Nation of Islam and changed his name to Muhammad Ali. A lot of people, especially most people in Jamestown, didn't think the heavyweight champion of the world should have a foreign-sounding name and they weren't hesitant about expressing their opinions. Especially in the "Letters to the Editor" section of The Jamestown Sun. Some of their writings were bad; most were awful.

But all that was overshadowed by my personal need for expedience. The train would be leaving in less than six minutes. It was time for positive, though perhaps unpopular, action.

"Muhammad Ali!" I hollered with as much sincerity as I could muster. "I'm a newspaper reporter," I yelled, using that term rather than "newspaper editor" on the assumption that if he did respond, he'd feel more comfortable speaking with a reporter because he was accustomed to dealing with sportswriters but probably had never been interviewed by an editor because editors somehow had acquired the reputation of being rather snooty with little time for such trivial matters as sports, particularly boxing.

As I pondered all this, a door directly in front of me opened and a giant stepped out. It was Muhammad Ali. And regardless of what his name was, he was enormous. He was the biggest human I had ever seen.

I gulped and wondered how to address someone that large. Even worse, I was afraid that if I did address him, my voice would squeak and I'd come off looking like a country hick right there in front of the heavyweight champion of the world. But he eased my fears with a smile, and said, "May I help you?" His voice was soft and gentle, not at all like the raucous bellowing he displayed after flooring Liston to win the title.

He invited us into his compartment, asked us to sit, and complimented us for finding him by using his new name. "Do you have some questions for me?" he inquired and I couldn't believe that this was the same person I had watched in the newsreels and television reruns, the belligerent young man crowing over his fallen opponent. So I asked him about that persona as opposed to the gentle giant sitting in front of me. "Do you know about Gorgeous George?" he responded. It was a surprising answer. Gorgeous George was a professional wrestler, known nationwide for being a mean, stinkin' rotten, vociferous, loud-mouthed braggart who cheated, wore his hair in long blonde tresses and sucker-punched his opponents when the ref wasn't looking. Since pro wrestling was big in North Dakota, everybody knew about Gorgeous George. And everybody hated him.

Ali smiled again. "When I was a boy," he said, "I watched him wrestle once and saw how much attention he got because of his attitude and I decided that's how I wanted people to respond."

I asked if it didn't bother him when people mistook his actions in the ring for his true nature. This time, his smile became a grin. "It's all an act," responded, almost gleefully. "Because of that, I don't take it personally. None of it means anything."

The champ agreed to pose for a photo, but before I could get my next question beyond my constricted throat and out of my arid mouth, he said, "Do you know the train's moving?"

The 3:17, obviously unaware of the epic news event being conducted in one of its passenger cars, was leaving town. So was Muhammad Ali. So were Wayne Deery and I.

This was, to say the least, a frightful situation. In an instant, our world became filled with drama, pathos, confusion, irregular thoughts, a large amount of illconcealed panic and the awful realization that since both Wayne's father and my dad worked for the railroad, whatever course of action we took next would be spread across their workplace faster than an errant spoonful of tomato sauce goes after the front of a white dinner jacket.

We gave Ali a hurried thanks and raced for an exit. Once there, we were assured by the passing landscape that the train was indeed moving. This left us with three choices:

First, we could jump off a moving train, like they did in the movies. When we saw how fast the train was already chugging out of Jamestown, we hastily decided against such action.

Second, we could ride it all the way to Bismarck, the next stop about 100 miles away, then try to figure out how to get home. It was not only an embarrassing solution, it would be costly. We'd probably have to spend the night in some fleabag motel and get ravaged by bedbugs. So that also became a non-option.

Third, we could pull the emergency cord to stop the train, jump off and try to sneak back into town without being noticed. Common sense dictated that this was the best plan so I yanked the cord. The train stopped about a half-mile later. We disembarked and walked the two miles back to the office in the hope that nobody'd notice.

It was a vain hope.

We never had a chance.

Everybody noticed.

Railroaders, by their very nature, believe that because they carry goods and passengers across the nation, they are also duty-bound to spread good news as fast as possible. And to them, this was good news. By the time we got back downtown, our adventure was common knowledge.

A Night With the Guitarists

An unexpected "two-fer-one" set of interviews took place on a trip to Nashville where I met and interviewed Waylon Jennings (top left), and Johnny Cash, (bottom right).

NASHVILLE, TENNESSEE – WHEN I first met Jim Branscum, he told me he'd been a faithful reader of my column for several years. Naturally, this made him an immediate appointee to my list of good friends.

Branscum was an artist and a very good one. He did exceptionally fine pencil sketches, then added sculpting to his repertoire. One of his sculptures was a bronze bust of Waylon Jennings, the internationally acclaimed country and western singing idol. It was commissioned by Jennings' wife, Jesse Coulter, also a country and western singer. Jennings liked the work so much that he asked Branscum if he'd give permission for it to appear on the cover of his upcoming album.

The artist readily accepted, and Jennings invited him to his home in Nashville for the unveiling of the album cover. And, being the good friend that he was, Branscum asked me to accompany him. It took some fast talking to convince my editors at *The Phoenix Gazette* that this was a newsworthy event but they eventually succumbed to my well-crafted logic and persistent whining.

Jennings' home wasn't hard to find because everyone from cab driver to flight attendant knew where it was. Just look for the biggest house in town, they advised, and that'll be it. They were right. It was an enormous house. I had lived in towns that were smaller.

There were hundreds of people there. I didn't know any of them except Jim Branscum. But I knew who a lot of them were – Waylon Jennings, Johnny Cash, Jesse Coulter, Little Jimmy Dickens, Tanya Tucker – so there I was, a little farm kid from North Dakota socializing with a houseful of country and western greats.

Life couldn't get much better.

But it did -- until it turned bad.

I was just standing there, clutching a free beer, when a voice in back of me said, "How ya doin', son?" The voice sounded like it had been dragged over gravel then smoothed with buckets of fine champagne. It was deep and it was mellow but it reflected hard times and misery, all in the same breath.

I knew that voice, so I turned around and Johnny Cash extended his hand and shook mine and every inch of my insides tangled themselves into one tremendous knot and the knot forced itself up into my throat. I tried to reply but no sound emerged. I wanted to say something country and western like, "How y'all doing' yerseff, Mr. Cash?" But nothing came out.

Finally, while trying to be cool while attempting to hold back a free-beer-inspired burp, I was able to respond. I said, "Hey, Johnny," like we'd known each other for years. But I said it in a squeaky voice that resembled used air escaping from a balloon that had been let loose before the opening was tied shut. In the seconds that followed, I prayed for invisibility. I prayed that somebody from "Star Trek" would suddenly appear and use a transporter to send me into the next galaxy. I prayed that all those years of hard living and guitar twanging had rendered Johnny Cash partially deaf so he couldn't hear me.

But no. He heard me. And he grinned at my discomfort and said I'd better have another beer. Then he reached across a table, grabbed one and handed it to me. "I'm doin' just fine, son," he said, "and thanks for askin'."

Somebody with a camera approached us and wondered if we'd like our picture taken together. Cash replied, "Well, if this gentleman don't mind, I sure don't." So we posed, then chatted for a while before he said he had to move on. "Nice talkin' to ya, son," he said as we parted. And I gathered the inner strength required to lower my voice down to about one degree below falsetto and responded, "Yup, sure was."

Later, while talking with Jennings, he asked where I was from. When I told him, he said Phoenix was one of his favorite cities, but he liked Tucson better. Then he added that since I had come all the way from Phoenix, I should partake in more of the free offerings. I accepted, and accepted way more than once. Because of my readiness to accept, it turned into one of those nights I'll never forget – if only I could remember it.

The beer flowed freely and I felt obligated, as the only newspaper columnist from Phoenix in attendance, to uphold the tradition of accepting freebies regardless of the circumstances. So I accepted and accepted, then accepted some more, then accepted one for the road, then accepted another one to help me get up enough courage to ask where the bathroom was.

The trip home wasn't much fun, especially when the plane encountered turbulence over Oklahoma. When I got to my office the next day, openly suffering from a severe case of the freebie flu, the editors mercifully said I didn't have to write a report because they had already published an Associated Press account of the event.

But they did suggest that if I felt as bad as I looked, I might write a first-person story about going to a hospital emergency room.

Part II: The Writing Life

By
Cecil F. Scaglione

*I left North Bay, Ontario, to find a place in
the world that wasn't friggin' freezin'...*

Editor's Note: *Cecil F. Scaglione is a native Canadian and naturalized American, who spent his six-decade long career first as a newspaper reporter than an award-winning public relations executive. For the past decade he has operated an international news syndicate, Mature Life Features, servicing more than 50 newspapers across the U.S., and Canada.*

Cecil Scaglione at the Windsor, Ontario Star

Reporters Make Strange Alliances

You get the opportunity to work and write for publications around the world once you've been admitted to the newspaper business.

I was fortunate to be a reporter. When not reporting, I was a copy editor, photo editor, composing room makeup editor, and administrative editor, among other roles.

But I have never been, nor ever wanted to be, a J O U R N A L I S T.

Capital J journalists claim to be digging for the truth. All the while, they toss aside facts they feel are not relevant to what they believe is the truth. So, they feed you their version of events, not a mirror of what happened or was said but what they feel was relevant.

I was set on what I've always believed to be the straight road in reporting by my first city editor.

Geoff Lane was an ex-Brit who spent his entire Canadian career at the *Sarnia Observer*, a daily newspaper in the Ontario city across from Port Huron, Mich., at the mouth of the St Clair River that drinks in Lake Huron.

My term there was only a few months but the lessons he crammed into my psyche loomed large over the years.

His first rule has been my conscious and conscience compass all through my career. It echoed a mantra repeated every high-school day by Rev. Dominic Kerwin in French class: "Don't believe anything you hear and only half of what you see."

It was on my third day on the job in Sarnia. I was returning to the newsroom from an assignment with photographer Doug Henderson when Geoff called me over to his desk and firmly, but in a friendly and fatherly fashion, said:

"Scag, people out there are paid to lie to you." Amen.

I never asked or was told what prompted that comment, but that rule still applies. Very few in today's news-gathering business are aware of it.

That terrible truth erupted just a few years ago while I was having fun free-lancing for a local newspaper. I covered some of the boards and commissions but did most of the feel-good stories that the Pulitzer Prize-hunting full-time staff couldn't stoop to do.

As a result, I got to meet and greet a broad cross-section of the populace in the cities we covered and picked up dribs and drabs of goings on from both the street folks and power-brokers..

During a chat with a 30-something City Hall reporter about one of the major issues coming up before the City Council, I thought I was sharing some intelligence gathered from some of the movers and shakers I canoodled with when it occurred to me that I was being patronized. I asked him, "Are you saying that the people I talk to are lying but the people you talk to are telling the truth?" Without a blink, he nodded his head and said, "Yeah."

That's when I quit working for that publication.

A major lesson along these lines surfaced decades earlier when I became a reporter for *Isvestia*, the Russian government's official mouthpiece.

It occurred back in the late '50s during a visit by Russia's national hockey team in the twin cities of Kitchener-Waterloo, about 60 miles east of Toronto.

This was during the era when the K-W Dutchman hockey team – so called because of the town's German origins and its heavy Pennsylvania Dutch–Amish population – were competing for and winning world-class titles.

And every Russian player worth his national-team uniform chopped up the ice like Detroit Red Wings Mr. Hockey -- Gordie Howe -- because he was the strongest and most efficient skater in the National Hockey League.

Accompanying the team was a gaggle of reporters we hosted at the K-W Press Club. During our chats, we learned from the *Isvestia* staffers that the closest interpretation they could produce for that title was "*Dispatch.*"

Like colleagues we've met from all corners of the globe, we got talking business, and a**hole editors and we wondered how they functioned under the heavy editorial anvil of the Russian government.

Dmitri (I've long forgotten his last name) shrugged us off by asking how many of our stories get printed that our editors didn't approve of. End of discussion because we didn't want to get into an argument.

The Russia-Canada game was scheduled for the next night and, a few hours before the game, Dmitri dropped by the *K-W Record* newsroom and asked for me. He said he'd been assigned to another story in another town and asked if I would call him after the game with the score and a few highlights.

Sure, I said, and called him after the game, which the Dutchmen won. After I give him the goals scored and the names of who scored and assisted, he asked for and got the crowd total, the tenor of the play, IDs of a few celebrities in the crowd, and a couple of other items.

And that was that,

I never saw any story. I never got paid. And never heard from him again. But I know I once was a reporter for *Isvestia*.

Memory's Music to My Ears

INTERVIEWING WORLD FIGURES AND CELEBRITIES is part of being a newsman – er, newsperson in today's PC environment.

But much of the behind-the-scenes stuff is more memorable than the in-ink or oncamera stuff.

Like Milton Berle asking where he could find a good cigar in town. Or Cliff Robertson looking for a shot of good scotch. Prince Philip wondering what locals eat. And Lester B. Pearson – Nobel Prize winner and Canadian Prime Minister at one time – seeking a ride back to his hotel.

One of the most rewarding memories that constantly bobs to the surface of a career that stretched over six decades is that of a musical group that most folks no longer remember.

It involves Jerry Murad and the Harmonicats – no, not the one with the midgets. His trio was filled out by Al Fiore and Don Les. They zoomed into the limelight in the late '40s with a million-selling rendition of "Peg 'O My Heart" and managed to remain visible with hit tunes until they disbanded shortly after the turn of this century.

Our first encounter occurred in the late '50s when the trio was one of the acts booked for the annual week-long fair in Kitchener, an industrial town about an hour west of Toronto, Ontario.

Part of my assignment for the week was covering the fair, always a fun job because there was no stress and we got to hang around with the exhibitors and entertainers. There wasn't much for the musicians to do during the day so we arranged golf games for them with my sports-writer buddy Ray Alviano. Both Jerry and Al spent the days on the links while Don had a diversion arranged in a nearby town.

As the week progressed we got to know and grow comfortable with one another and Jerry and Al would join our group at the K-W Press Club after their gig and while away the rest of the night. Don had his diversion.

We were the only married couple in our group so we usually held a Saturday night BYOL soiree at your house, which we rented and had a sizeable recreation room in the basement. Everyone has one back east, because they have to find a use for their basements.

We invited the Harmonicats to join us after the show. I was on duty on the premises so I drove them – Don ducked out to his diversion -- to our party and they blended in smoothly.

Suddenly, everything went quiet as Jerry and Al slid into their "Peg 'O My Heart" serenade to my then wife, Peg.

I still get chills recalling that moment when these folks who had become friends played their memorable tune in the basement of my little house in Kitchener.

An epilogue occurred a few years later, when the trio was headlining at Detroit's major night club, The Roostertail. The iconic complex is still owned by the Schoenith family, which includes brothers Lee and Jerry, who were hydroplane boat racers.

Jerry Murad called me at my desk in the Windsor Star (across the Detroit River from Detroit) and said, "I heard you moved to Windsor and we're going be at the Roostertail next week so why don't you and Peg come catch the show."

Great, I thought, and we picked a night. We chose a week night so the place wouldn't be too packed and arranged to pick him up at his downtown Detroit hotel and drive him up to the riverside nightclub

It was a cold winter night. I had a moth-eaten old maroon Mercury at the time with the floor on the passenger side eaten away by rust. Jerry and Peg sat in the back to stay warm.

The doorman at the club was not too pleased to see this piece of junk approach and looked like he was about to thumb us out of the property.

But the back door opened and, when he recognized Jerry Murad, he had no choice but to back down when the show's headliner said:

"Could you please park Mr. Scaglione's car until we're through with the show." That moment ranks pre high in my memory bank, too.

My First Major Story

ASK ANY NEWSHOUND WHICH WAS their most-memorable story and you'll probably hear of a disaster – the Titanic, the Hindenberg, the Twin Tower.

My first most-memorable (there have been a couple more since imprinted in my brain) was the collapse of the Listowel Memorial Arena in the small mill town on the outskirts of the Ahmish farming country in Southwestern Ontario. Photographer Dick Sutton and I had no idea of the scope and seriousness of the incident as we raced the 35 miles from the *Kitchener-Waterloo Record* newsroom to what would become a permanent scar in the small community. (Listowel was populated with a few thousand people but it seemed smaller than that both at the time and in recollection.)

Seven young hockey players aged 10 to 12 who were scrimmaging in the rink were killed along with their coach. Seven other kids and another adult were taken and admitted to hospital. Nine other people were treated and released from hospital throughout the day – Saturday, Feb. 28, 1959.

Eight other children and adults in the structure escaped injury. They had been in the lobby or one of the dressing rooms when what sounded like "a giant garage door slamming shut" reverberated throughout the community at 9:20 a.m. A father watched the tons of wood and iron crush his child. A player running late for practice was blown back out of the lobby just as he rushed in the front door. A months-later inquiry cited poor construction as a root of the disaster. The building was only four years old. It had been erected by mostly volunteer labor and shoddy work was reportedly uncovered in some of the laminated trusses and footings of support columns.

This was aggravated by a heavy load of snow on the roof that was made heavier by recent rainfall.

Veteran sports editor Len Taylor had raced to the scene before anyone else and was dictating a story to one of our rewrite editors by a phone he had managed to corral in one of the stores along Main Street. We found his car, which led us to him.

As soon as he finished talking, he took charge and headed to the wreckage so all of us would have an idea of the task ahead of us. Then we regrouped in a small eatery to plan our next moves.

Len doled out assignments quickly. Reporter Hank Koch and another photographer were given the "prize" chore – get pictures and background stories and quotes from the families of the fatalities.

Dick and I were to do the same with anyone else who was in the building, placing priority on those still in hospital. First we had to get their names and addresses. All of us were to harvest any and all "color" material about the building, the families, the town – everything. This was an international story. Papers as far away as Holland and New Zealand carried the story.

As news teams from everywhere gathered, it was decided to establish a pool – a center where photos could be developed and statistics collected to share amongst each other. The Record stringer (correspondent) in Listowel arranged with his boss to use the offices of the weekly *Listowel Banner*.

Our team – there were seven of us – arranged to meet at meal times in the diner where Len had handed out our chores. It was the standard mom-and-pop homecooked type of eatery that every small town has. That Saturday evening, the hot beef sandwich was menu'd at $1.49.

The following day, as herds of newspaper, radio, television and magazine writers, reporters and photographers and looky-loos converged on the town, the hot beef sandwich was $11.49. Easy to insert a "1" to the price.

Another lesson was learned that same day. The pool system was working. Names, ages and addresses of everyone were collected and checked and rechecked. The history of the town was compiled and copied for everyone to collect.

Photographers dumped their rolls of film to be developed and printed and prints deemed "public property" by the shooter were shared.

Until word got out that the *Toronto Star* team had thieved a half dozen rolls of undeveloped film. Len took charge and called the Ontario Provincial Police and reported the theft by a trio driving a late-model vehicle with Toronto Star painted plainly all over it.

The car was stopped on the freeway short of Toronto and the Star was forced to pay for a cab to carry the film back to Listowel. We heard later that, instead of any sort of reprimand, the film filchers were given an attaboy by their editors for their ingenuity under pressure.

Sunday melted into Monday, which was bulletined around town as the Official Day of Mourning. After capturing snaps of survivors and family members entering and coming out of churches all day, it was time to return to the mundane. I never got back to Listowel after that Monday.

But those three days are vivid in my brain.

I remember everything being gray.

Catching Up with Political Prattle

IT ISN'T EVERY DAY ONE gets the opportunity to tell the man who once was arguably the third-most powerful politician on the globe that he did wrong.

It harked back to when I was about 12 and heading over to my then-friends home a five-minute walk from my home in the east end of North Bay, a railroad town some 220 miles north of Toronto.

The government of Canada had initiated a children's allowance program a couple of years earlier.

Having sold the *North Bay Daily Nugget* on the streets of this railroad town, I had become an avid reader and followed the reasons for and repercussions of what I learned later was Canada's first universal welfare program.

It began with monthly payments of $5 for each child under 5 years of age, $6 for those 6 to 9, $7 for each aged 10 to 12, and $8 for those 13 to 15.

The program was born out of studies during the 1920s in the United Kingdom, Australia, United States and Canada prompted by the premise that what may be a living wage to an employee who is single may be below the poverty level for a married worker.

The children's allowance payments were instituted to help close that gap for poor families, the politicians declared.

Opponents argued that this family allowance, which was given to every family, was a sop to voters in French Canada, where many-children households tended to be more frequent than the rest of the Dominion.

I was thinking about that as I walked to my friends' house. It was a French-Canadian family. The lady of the house gave birth to 22 children. That was not unusual in our town. And eight of them still qualified for the monthly assistance payments.

The income was enough to make the mortgage payments on their house with money left over for groceries, or whatever.

This was by no means a poor family. Their father was a railroad engineer making a healthy salary well above that of the lowly section-hands like my father, who the government sent $13 a month for my brother and me.

So my first political science lesson was that the Canadian government was lying about claiming this program was devised and designed to lift families out of poverty. Among the politicians leading this phalanx was Health and Welfare Minister Paul Martin. He was elected to Parliament for more than three decades by voters in Windsor, Ontario, the bustling neighbor of Detroit across the river that drains Lake St. Clair into Lake Erie.

That's where I got the opportunity to point out that his welfare program wasn't like we were told.

I had joined the staff of the *Windsor Star* and Paul – everyone called him Paul – dropped by the newsroom regularly and made it a point to make his office and staff in Ottawa open and accessible anytime anyone from the staff visited the nation's capital, whether for work or for play.

He was the compleat politician. One afternoon on our rounds, a staff photographer and I drove by his home in Windsor's comfortable quarter of Walkerville and spotted him and Dean Rusk seated in the lee of his multi-story brick manse nestled among the massive trees populating his grounds. We honked and he waved us in to have lemonade and chat with him and the U.S. Secretary of State.

It gave us a photo and a bit of a color story about our visit with a couple if the world's leading diplomats (Paul was Rusk's Canadian counterpart as Minister of External Affairs as well as delegate to the United Nations at the time).

It was during this period that he became one of the world's most powerful politicians.

He was sitting in for U Thant, UN secretary general, who was out of service on a special diplomatic mission, putting Paul in the third-most powerful chair behind Russia's secretary general and the U.S. president.

It was while camped in one of his campaign cars with him during a re-election drive that I buttonholed him about the political propaganda I had grown wise to as a pre-teen.

He just smiled and wagged his head and finger and said, "Oh, Cecil, Cecil, but don't you know that we're giving these children much more now so we don't have to worry about them being needy."

Before I had the opportunity to claim that was more political propaganda and prattle, he asked me if I could run into the store coming up at the corner to get him a cigar. You see, he never carried any money on him. Not a penny. That was OK because I put the item on my expense account.

Praise Preferred

COMPLIMENTS ARE HARD TO COME by in any business.

We get to hear complaints and criticism loudly in the news business. Sometimes we even deserve them.

But compliments? They're so few and far between, we recall them in full color. An easy one to pull up is a quick glimpse of the late Rex McInnes who was sitting in the City Desk at the *Windsor Star* when he "suggested" I accompany a photographer to a hi-tech conference at a local college and get cutlines – identities of the folks who appear in the photo.

We returned to the newsroom about 90 minutes later and, while waiting for the photog to soup and develop the film and photos, I bashed out an essay designed to show the reader how the psychobabble about polymers – the subject of the conference – affected us but no one realized how much.

It took seven minutes. I tossed it at Rex to show him what we had just wasted our time on.

As I returned to my desk after getting a coffee refill, I heard Rex snickering – he never laughed, he had this infectious snicker – and he muttered, loud enough for me to hear:

"This is pretty damn good, Scag."

He thought it was good enough to publish and it won a massive and major Canadian award for humor writing.

You can't get a much bigger compliment than that.

The comment by Findlay G. Stewart, moderator of the Presbyterian Church of Canada at the time, ranks high in my short list of compliments.

At the time, I was church editor at the *Kitchener–Waterloo Record*, the Southwestern Ontario twin-city daily newspaper about an hour out of Toronto. We put out a page of church news and interviews once a week. It was a rather important page because the K-W region was a hub of church views with leaders of several denominations based there.

As news developed, calling "Fin" Stewart at his office in the imposing St. Andrew's Presbyterian Church just a block up the street from the Record building was a regular part of the job. The mustached, jovial and rotund cleric often strolled his imposing figure down to visit our newsroom.

Leo Laderoute, an old friend from my hometown and a fellow ballplayer, hung around with Fin Stewart's son when he went carousing. One day, he pulled me aside and said, "Ol' Fin wants me to tell you something -- for being a Catholic kid, you know a lot about all those other religions."

I debated thanking the prelate for his kind and supportive words, but decided not to since he chose to deliver the compliment via messenger. So, I responded the same way.

I forgot to ask Leo if he ever delivered it.

Which leads to a third kudo that was much appreciated.

In involves Leo because we were on the same team in a couple of softball leagues. And we used to gather for outlaw games on Sundays because we rarely were scheduled for regular games then.

These were fun games that attracted top players from throughout the region. One Sunday we arranged for a group of Kitchener-Waterloo Press Club pickup players to play the professional football Hamilton Tiger Cats team, along with whatever pick-up players they could get.

We had a particularly quick and blazing whip-arm pitcher named Wayne Rehkopf along with National Hockey League Hall of Famer Bill Durnan, who was one of the all-time great orthodox pitchers.

I was the catcher.

A long-time and active member of the Press Club was Bob Rafferty, who coached the K-W Dutchmen during their championship and Olympic hockey years in the mid-fifties.

He, like most of the couple hundred folks who built our spectator crowd, enjoyed the sauce more than the spectacle as the Sunday wore on.

Finally, as we claimed the bench for our turn at bat in the sixth inning, he sat down beside me, slapped my thigh and said, "You know, Scag, I thought you were too small, but you're a helluvan athlete. Yep, you're an athlete," and tottered off. I don't recall playing any better that day, but I felt a lot better after that.

Writing History

NEWSPAPERS HAVE BEEN CALLED THE first rough draft of history. Reporters dish out those drafts. Some change history.

One of the earliest history makers in my collection of first drafts poured out of my typewriter in the late '50s.

It was brief paragraph in a roundup of local items pulled from the police blotter on Easter Sunday. The item pertinent to this tale cited a father being charged with contributing to the delinquency of a minor.

A neighbor reported to police that he had served his young daughter – she was about 10 at the time -- a glass of wine as the family gathered for Easter dinner around her grandparent's backyard picnic table under a balmy springtime sun.

When the accused was arraigned that Monday, his lawyer urged leniency because the action was nothing more than acceptable family behavior at such festive occasions.

As it turned out, the gent broke several laws. Not only did he give a minor an alcoholic drink, he gave someone other than himself a drink while not in his domicile, since the misdemeanor occurred at his parents' house, and he gave alcohol to someone who didn't live there.

Sounds complicated, doesn't it?

This little event blew apart dozens of arcane blue laws that governed the acquisition and consumption of alcohol throughout Canada's largest province.

The man responsible for pulling the trigger to shoot down those laws was Crown Attorney Harold Daufman, the U.S. district attorney counterpart in the Southern Ontario city of Kitchener a few miles over the western horizon from Toronto.

Daufman prosecuted the case with his usual vigor. The guilty party pleaded not guilty to breaking the law but admitted giving his daughter the wine, which his court-appointed lawyer emphasized was customary on such festive occasions in his client's homeland.

The verdict was guilty on both counts of serving liquor to a minor and serving liquor to someone while not in his domicile and a fine levied.

When the magistrate – equivalent of a municipal judge in the U.S. – rapped up the case with his gavel, Daufman asked for a recess, took the confused and convicted father by elbow, and walked him out of the courtroom. He grabbed him and his attorney by their lapels and told them to appeal the conviction because the laws he'd just fought to uphold were absurd.

The defense attorney agreed with the attitude and action proposed. To help persuade the still-addled father who was convicted of contributing to the delinquency of his child, the lawyer added that he'd do the work pro bono – for free – to help untangle the twisted legal views of demon rum.

As details of the incident were picked up by news organizations and politicians across the country, the appeal process picked up speed. It too only a few months to have the appeal heard. And the convictions overturned.

This meant you could give someone a drink in your own home – something you couldn't do before.

Up till then, not only had it been illegal for me to give someone other than members of my immediate family who lived with me a drink in my house, nobody could bring their own alcohol to drink while visiting in my house because it was illegal to drink any liquor outside of their residence.

Alcohol of any sort -- beer, wine or liquor -- could not be served in restaurants because of the all- encompassing laws requiring everyone to drink at home or in designated licensed hotel quarters.

And never on Sundays.

Until that case shattered the Puritanical atmosphere promoted by prohibitionists, there was nowhere to legally buy alcohol or drink it publicly between midnight Saturday and noon Monday.

These and ancillary anti-alcohol laws, which were routinely ignored by most adults as they went about their daily lives, were crushed out of existence as the entire column of blue laws began crumbling rapidly as lawmakers clambered aboard the blast-the-blue-laws bandwagon.

Everyone at that Easter dinner around the backyard picnic table had been breaking the law.

We never did find out how the neighbor who reported the infraction felt about pioneering the enlightened liquor laws for millions of Ontario residents.

Part III: The People You Meet

By
John Beatty

"I come from Missouri where not all Jackasses are mules"

Editor's Note: *John Beatty is an award-winning long-time radio and television personality from the Midwest. He got his start in the U.S. Air Force working with the American Forces*

Network (AFN) in Germany, then worked for a number stations in Kansas and Missouri, including WIBW in Topeka, WDAF in Kansas City, and KYW All News Radio in Philadelphia. He spent most of his career, 35 years, with KOGO (now KGTV) in San Diego where he was news anchor, reporter, documentary producer and host, as well as the station's editorial director.

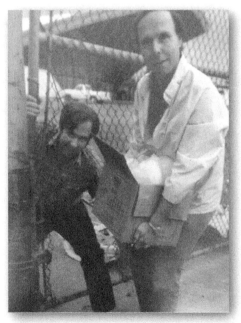

Circa 1981: Morrow and Beatty carrying "supplies" through a fence at the Mexican border in Tijuana, Baja Norte

Taking a Bath During a GOP Convention

WHILE WORKING AS A TV reporter in Topeka, Kansas I often spoke with fella named Henry Bubb. At that time he was chairman of the area's largest Savings & Loan Association. As the 1964 GOP campaigns approached he reminisced about an interesting and valuable personal connection he had made 24 years earlier.

Bubb had been an active Young Republican, and it found him deeply involved in the GOP's 1940 convention nomination. His activities for the Republicans took time away from his work and some wondered whether he should keep his executive position. But the politics was important to him, so, he stayed the course.

He told of the hard scramble to get Wendell Willkie as the 1940 Presidential nominee. He and another young fella went so far as to walk GOP delegates past the hotel room bathtub as Willkie cleaned up.

Willkie, who had been a Democrat-turn Republican, won the nomination, but lost the election. However, the Indiana lawyer so impressed President Roosevelt, he ended up an FDR friend and served as an envoy by going to England to assess the looming war with Germany. After the election, Bubb's S&L was facing some problems with the government. Bubb had mentioned to friends that his position might be in jeopardy. The word went up the line and came back from Washington, D.C.: "Keep Bubb and your problems can be solved." In 1941 at age 34, Henry Bubb was named the S&L's president.

And, that other fella helping Bubb parade GOP delegates past Willkie's bathtub? A guy from Illinois named Everett Dirksen.

'C'mon, guys, just let me in.'

It was a bright sunny fall day in San Diego (really, is there any other kind?) and the University of San Diego campus was in controlled frenzy. The 1996 presidential campaigns were at top pitch. USD was going to get a piece of the action.

San Diego had been host to that year's GOP convention. The Republican delegates had picked Senator Bob Dole of Kansas as their standard bearer. And at their convention in Chicago Democrats renominated President Bill Clinton.

It was a campaign pitting the highly-decorated WWII veteran Dole, who was the leading Republican in the U.S. Senate against a popular incumbent with a flair for campaigning.

But what had the USD folks worked up was the pending presidential appearances on campus. The candidates staging a debate right on campus before a television audience of millions.

Students had variety of assignments, including media folks like me. TV trucks parked in their assigned area. Debate credentials had been issued to people who had passed the official security clearances. News folks were busy chasing predebate stories. But on the day of the debate the security perimeter was tightened.

The US. Secret Service expanded its presence. And credentials were required. It was into this phalanx of security that Police Chief Jerry Sanders drove his unmarked car onto campus. His security liaison, Capt. David Bejarano, was busy elsewhere as Secret Service agents blocked his progress. Surely, they reasoned the police chief would have a driver.

Sanders told the agents to just give the USD police chief a call. "You guys are working with her," the chief explained. They made the call and she validated him as chief -- USD Chief Rana Sampson knew alright. She was and is Chief Sanders' wife.

Remembering The 'Little Guy!'

IN THE MID-1980's I WAS reporting producing documentaries at KGTV10. With some spare time on my hands one afternoon, the director I often worked with asked me if I'd like to go along on a public service announcement with Ray Kroc. Well of course I would. Like many San Diegans I was eager to see this multimillionaire food merchant and Padres owner up close and personal.

After all he had personally saved the Padres for San Diego. Another deal to move the Padres to Washington had fallen through. Kroc had built a fortune and now he wanted a baseball team. As the story goes he had a top assistant call the club, offering to buy it. General Manager Buzzi Bavasi reportedly asked "Who's your group?" Mr. Kroc Is the group, and so Ray Kroc plunked down $12 million of his own bucks for a baseball team.

In a recent 2017 film, **The Founder**, Michael Keaton has done a pretty good job of portraying the essence of master salesman Ray Kroc. Physically he was shorter than Keaton but certainly made up for it in other ways.

America knows him as the man who revolutionized drive-in eating with MacDonald's. Although the movie is named "**The Founder**," "**The Takeover Guy**" would work.

But for San Diegans Ray Kroc would always be remembered as the outspoken owner of the Padres baseball team. And he believed the folks who bought the tickets deserved good entertainment. That is, a team that wins!

A bit sauced opening night 1974, and with his Padres losing badly, an emotional Kroc took over the stadium public address mike and apologized to the fans for lousy play

Major League Baseball officials didn't like it, fined him for his actions but the fans loved it.

Bob Chandler, a member of the broadcast team, said he could always tell when Kroc was in town. As he passed a certain McDonald's on the way to the stadium the owner would be busy polishing the windows.

This is the guy I wanted to see.

We got to the stadium and setup. Soon we heard Kroc railing at GM Bavasi about changes or improvements he had asked for but didn't see. He then saw us, we introduced ourselves, and he asked "What do you want me to do?" We told him. He did it smoothly and graciously thanked us for effort. He then went back to telling Bavasi what he wanted done.

Kroc's secretary who had walked out with him told me this story about Ray Kroc:

The manager of a Little League in Santee had sent Ray Kroc a letter asking for his support. Among hundreds, if not thousands his Chicago office received And filtered every day, this one got through.

Kroc approved the request, and from then on the Santee manager had only to ask the San Diego Padres for what he needed and he would receive.

That's the good Ray Kroc remembering the little guy.

Getting 'Buzzed' While Changing the Guard

IT WAS A COMFORTABLY WARM sunny day outside Wurzburg, Germany. Sitting at a table overlooking the U. S. Army's 1st Infantry Division parade ground. Troops were marching in.

I was an oddity. An Airman First Class among army majors colonels, a star or two, and captain or two as well. We, and colleague Fran McLaughln, on a rise to observe military pageantry at its finest, a major change of command.

Fran McLaughlin was Program Director, (a Department of the Army civilian employee) and me, an announcer, for the American Forces Network radio station AFN Nuremburg. We were there to prepare to broadcast the ceremonies the following day.

The First Infantry Division, "The Big Red One", was the longest surviving Unit in our army, initially formed as the 1st Expeditionary Force for World War I. Reorganized as the First Infantry Division it stormed ashore on Omaha Beach on D-Day.

It was very military proud. Ranks filled with Regular Army soldiers, Regular Army, not just draftees. Much was expected. Much was delivered. Just look at its battle honors. But now it was a big fist in the Cold War to help prevent any Russian moves. Military units in Germany devoted a lot of their time on field exercises, often coinciding with similar exercises by Russian troops. Each side wondering if this time is the real thing.

But not on this day. No, this was an exercise in parade discipline.

And Maj. Gen. Charles Lanham, preparing to turn over his command, wanted all to look and be "Army Sharp."

For an Airman First Class it was something to see and feel. The army officers next us were not at all impressed with a young Air Force enlisted man broadcasting. After all earlier in their careers it had been the "Army" Air Corps and army enlisted/commissioned ranks just didn't mix. I must admit whatever discomfort or disdain my presence might have caused was a secret delight. There was some of it in the US Air Force but usually not as pronounced.

Then, as the general was starting to address the troops, a US Air Force plane buzzed the field. The general looked up and you could see he was annoyed, but kept on talking. But the plane buzzed again but much lower. Now the general was angry as the plane came over one more time. It appeared determined to disrupt what the general was doing. And, well, the troops were a little shaky, and starting to break formation on their own. Soon the field was clear and the plane landed.

A few words were spoken, the aircrew and medics loaded a severely burned patient on board and the air evac plane took off.

The next day the ceremony went on as planned with a cool crisp broadcast.

And one Airman First Class hiding a big smirk.

'The Outrageous Hero'

His sister called him the "Outrageous Hero." He was described as "Bold, Profane, and utterly Outrageous." The only person I ever knew who had a men's room named in his honor. A nun who taught him in school said "he was the orneriest son-of-bitch I ever loved."

Brien Thomas Collins. Just B.T. to those who knew him. Or "Captain Hook." He was all of that and more. A hard drinker who had heart problems.

An acquaintance had steered him to me to appear on my weekly TV interview show. I had heard about this guy. Former Green Beret Captain, who lost an arm and a leg in Vietnam. He mishandled his own grenade during an attack, spent 18 months in military hospitals and would deal with pain the rest of his life. At a banquet years later a kid sitting across the table asked about the hook/ claw he sees for a right hand. Collins quickly whipped it off and slid it across the table so the youngster could see for himself.

He went to Santa Clara University, and its law school. Why? "Shortest distance between two buildings on campus," B.T. would explain. Years later the folks who run the university wanted to name an office in his honor. He said, "No, name the men's room in the law library. 'The B.T. Collins Memorial Latrine,'" So, they did. That was B.T.

So, one day into the TV station comes this man limping on a prosthetic leg and gesturing with his prosthetic hook attached to his prosthetic arm. And eager to talk. He was director of the California Conservation Corps (CCC).

After law school, Collins tried practicing it didn't like it and with the help of a professor became a legislative liaison on Gov. Jerry Brown's staff. When asked by Brown if he had voted for him, B.T. famously replied "I never vote for short ex-Jesuits." B.T.'s quip didn't bother Brown. He impressed the governor with his ability to get passage of Brown's bills. With a whip-smart mind and mouth, and exuding charm, Collins worked the State Assembly, assigning profane or obscene names to many members. He said he could get by with it because "nobody would hit a one-armed man." Truth is they were honored to be so noted. He referred to the assembly as an Adult Daycare Center. And they loved it.

So, when Governor Brown wanted to appoint a new director for the poor- performing CCC, B.T. Collins was his man. Collins told me his approach was "My way or hit the highway." And that included "No Drugs!" The CCC offered jobs to young men working on state-owned lands and helping fight fires. Collins motto, which. still stands, is: "Hard Work, Low Pay, Miserable Conditions," But he also urged them to take educational classes to better themselves.

The half-hour TV interview taping flew by. His charm and smarts won us over. He would be back several times.

He would become Brown's chief of staff, and later Gov. Pete Wilson would appoint him to head the California Youth Authority. B.T. told me more than twodozen of his staffers had been gang members; he wanted to learn how they turned their lives around. Again, classic B.T., he sought answers and solutions.

B.T. would later be appointed and elected to the State Assembly. He had finally given up alcohol and would note on one of his campaign newsletters, how much campaign money he was saving. He was the spirit and chief fundraiser for Vietnam Memorial on the Capitol grounds and insisted it include a nurse.

He would die at 52, after two nearly back-to-back heart attacks as he prepared to speak at a luncheon. B.T. Collins was given a state funeral -- his body lying in state in the state Capitol. Thousand, including three governors, attended the memorial service.

But my memory is delighted by this story he told me. A San Diego financial guy had a problem with a certain state agency. He called the state's Business and Transportation Secretary whom he knew. She referred him to the governor's office and Chief of Staff B. T. Collins. The financial guy made an appointment and walked in. Seeing B.T. for the first time did grab his attention.

The financial guy explained his plight as Collins listened carefully. Then Collins picked up the phone, called the agency and told them to solve the problem. Pronto! The financial guy was nearly taken aback, but then Collins leaned in and said "Don't you tell anybody about this." The guy left the meeting happy.

Collins told me that story a few days later. Then an account of what had transpired appeared in a widely-read newspaper. The San Diegan quickly called B.T. to assure him he hadn't tipped anyone. B.T. laughed and said "I know, I leaked it." And, then said to him, and later to me, "wasn't that clever?" He was still chuckling and smiling. Enjoying helping people. That was the real B.T. Collins

Charles Who?

MENTION THE NAME "CHARLES COLSON" today and you might get just a blank stare. "Who?" Others might think "Nixon, Watergate, something from then." And some might say President Nixon's special counsel, who served prison time for obstructing justice in the break-in at the office of Daniel Elberg's psychiatrist hoping for information to discredit the man who leaked the Pentagon Papers.

Colson was that and more. A lawyer and ex-Marine, Colson had worked on numerous Republican campaigns. So, he was familiar with politics.

On President Nixon's staff he developed a reputation as someone "ruthless to get things done." "Grab 'em by the balls and their hearts and minds will follow," he would say. His fingerprints were all over the president's 'Plumbers Unit', so-called because it was formed to stop information leaks.

He would almost proudly say "he would walk over his grandmother" to get President Nixon elected. He suggested bombing a liberal Washington D.C think tank, and while firefighters were systematically trying to save the files, he'd grab them for possible info to use against them. It didn't happen, just an idea.

But with the collapse of the Watergate break-in, and the Pentagon Papers escapade, Colson became one of several Nixon aides to serve prison time, However, his prison time. seven months, was much different from the others.

Charles Colson became an Evangelical Christian in prison. He organized a Prison Fellowship preaching the gospel behind prison walls.

After release he wrote a book about it, "Born Again," and on a book tour stopped in San Diego. I scheduled an appearance on my "Newsmakers," a weekly news interview program I hosted along two other reporters.

The program moved right along and nothing historically memorable was said. But as we sat down on the set, Colson reached into a coat pocket and pulled out a card. He carefully wrote our names and then put it under his right thigh. One of us would ask a question and he would casually and quickly glance down and say "well John," or "well Rob" and so on. Just a bit of a personal touch, done smoothly and which made him look good. And the questioner just a bit proud that he 'knew' our names. Charles Colson was a thorough fella.

Morrow, Scaglione and Beatty on a break.

Part IV: True Tales From The Greatest Generation

By
Tom Morrow

"I left Iowa when I realized there was a big world out there that needed to be discovered."

Thomas J. Morrow, Sam Lowe, Cecil F. Scaglione and John Beatty

Editor's Note: *During the more than 20 years of writing feature stories and reporting for a daily newspaper in Oceanside, California, Tom Morrow was able interview a wide variety of World War II veterans – many of them highly decorated heroes. Arguably, there are more armed forces veterans, both active and retired living in San Diego County than anywhere else in the U.S. Sadly, most of the World War II veterans have passed on. The following stories a few of the gems Morrow captured.*

A Song of the Desert, Italian Style

CARLSBAD'S MURRAY DAVISON, WHO PASSED away in 2005, recalled his days back during World War II when he was a special services musician with the 9th Army Air Corps in North Africa. His first "gig" was Cairo in November 1942 when his band performed for members of the U.S. Air Corps and the British 8th Army.

But it was when he became a front-line entertainer, following the British army west after Field Marshal Bernard Montgomery won the first major victory against the "Desert Fox," Germany's Field Marshal Erwin Rommel and his Afrika Korps that Davison proved being in the band meant more to the war effort than just playing music and entertaining the troops.

"We took basic training and learned how to fight just like regular soldiers," he recalled.

After the fall of Tunis in June 1943, Davison's 17-member orchestra traveled across North Africa in a small convoy consisting of two command cars, a jeep and a "deuce-and-a-half" (2 1/2-ton truck).

"I was driving the lead vehicle, a command car, down this lonely road in the middle of the desert when suddenly we came upon a heavily-armed force of 300 Italian soldiers," Davison said with vivid recollection.

"We all thought we were dead -- we were scared to death, but then we spotted a white flag."

Murray said the Italians were all on foot, except for a small Fiat sports car that a couple of the officers were driving.

"They gave us the Fiat and an Italian major handed over his Beretta automatic pistol to me, which I still have," said Davison. "Those guys were starving. We fed them all our rations and then we headed for the nearest British Army base."

When our boys in the band showed up at the front gate of the British Army installation with 300 enemy prisoners, the colonel in charge couldn't believe his eyes.

"The Italians had been deserted by the Germans. The 'eye-ties' hated the Germans for having been treated with contempt by their supposed ally," Davison explained. "They told us they were more than delighted to be 'captured' by the Americans."

Davison said he and the band got a unit citation for the "capture" of the 300 Italians.

"No kidding. We were written up in *Yank* magazine, as well as *Stars & Stripes* newspaper," he laughed.

And, to think, the enemy surrendered to Davison's band without first hearing them play.

Loved ones didn't quite get the POW picture

2nd Lt. Jack Kellogg, B-17 co-pilot, spent the last few months of World War II in Stalag III. It was the POW camp made famous by the Hollywood film "The Great Escape."

Jack passed on a few years back, but while he was he, a great contribution from a different angle to the history of the war

SOME OF THE LOGBOOK ENTRIES of 2nd Lt. Jack Kellogg, a B-17 copilot made while he was a prisoner of war at Stalag Luft III would be of historical, albeit blackhumored, interest.

"During my first two months as a POW, I shared a small room with six RAF officers," Kellogg recalled. "There were many English flyers who had been incarcerated at Luft III for as long as four years.

He said daily German propaganda radio broadcasts beamed to Great Britain told English listeners how "fabulous" life was behind the barbed wires of a POW camp, describing it as a carefree life, consisting of frequent visits to area German tourist attractions.

Kellogg found some of the letters from British wives, fiancées, lovers and family members were just a tad on the naive side, so he jotted down a few excerpts from dozens of letters:

"I am so glad you got shot down before flying became really dangerous."

"It must be wonderful for you to get away to holiday camps, enjoy cinemas and those lovely long walks we read about in the paper."

"I suppose you are able to get the hometown newspapers."

"I enclosed some lovely mince pies but the Red Cross sent them back."

"I read in a POW magazine that Kriegies (prisoners) dream only of food. It that right?"

"It seems almost incredible that you should be in the heart of Germany but you are, aren't you?"

"It's the same dull routine these days. Work in the a.m., come home, go to a dance or a cinema. It's so monotonous. Still, I suppose there are a few things you do without too, so I have to do two weeks in the hospital and I can't blame you this time."

"I'm getting married on the 29th so please think kindly of me on that day and wish me well." -- an ex-fiancee

"I hope you will not return passion dead. Glad you are having a rest. Personally, I'm working night and day. Did I tell you I got married recently." -- an ex-fiancee

"Hurry up and get back. When you do, you will be in the money and I'll be in the mood. I married your brother and I am so happy to be in your family as I will be able to see you often." -- an ex-fiancee

"It is not very nice to be a prisoner-of-war, but it is honorable. I am having an affair with a Canadian airman and he is having cigarettes sent to you from Canada."-- a wife

"It's strange when one is flying, one's cares and troubles are forgotten."

"You must stop writing to John. He has been dead for two years."

"Your kit (duffle bag) arrived home and the first thing I saw when looking through it was a lot of photos of ugly-looking girls."

"I am not sending you any photos as they will just make you homesick."

"Try to get to Dresden and have a look at the picture gallery. The Boomadonna is worth seeing."

"As you asked for a half-dozen pairs of socks in every letter, I must presume you are joking, so I am sending you pajamas."

Going Ashore on D-day Plus 1

THE LATE JEROME V. "JERRY" Stapp, III, joined the U.S. Army in 1942. After a year of training, then 18-years-old, the Los Angeles native ended up at the Brooklyn Naval Shipyards for debarkation to Great Britain.

Once the troops had all of their equipment loaded onto the ship, Stapp, who was a buck sergeant (three stripes) and his men began their long journey across the Atlantic to Glasgow, Scotland. During peacetime, an ocean crossing trip to the British Isles from the East coast of the United States would take no more than five days. But, during World War II, with "wolf packs" of Nazi submarines lurking in the North Atlantic, the convoy would take up to 31 days.

As Stapp recalls that wartime journey, "Most of us (Army) guys were seasick throughout the voyage."

The ships were unloaded in Glasgow and re-loaded onto British Rail flatcars. "We rode out in the open on the flatcars all the way to south Wales where we would spend more weeks of training," Stapp recalled. "We were preparing for something big, but could only guess what it would be." For the next several weeks, Stapp's unit trained on the beaches of south Wales. "We knew something big was coming and we knew that our time in Great Britain was limited," he said. "We knew were being trained to fight in Europe."

In a matter of weeks, equipment and men were loaded once again onto ships berthed along the south coast of England.

"We were preparing for the largest amphibious assault in the history of the world," Stapp said. "We didn't know where we were going or exactly when it was to be, but, as it turned out, the big show was to be D-day, the sixth of June."

Stapp's unit, which consisted of half-tracks and amphibious tanks, was assigned to 12th Army Group, which was directly under Gen. Dwight D. Eisenhower, who was Supreme Allied Commander for the invasion of Europe. "We didn't go onto the beaches at Normandy that first day," Stapp recalled. "We landed the next day, June 7, 1944." "I was squad leader on a half-track," Stapp said. "I rode ashore on the half-track.

Our amphibious tanks didn't work so well. They were equipped with 37 mm cannons, which were popguns compared to the big 88 mm guns on the German tiger tanks we would be facing."

Two of the amphibious tanks sunk before reaching shore.

"During the Battle of San Lo a few days later, the other two tanks stalled trying to climb a hill," Stapp recalled.

After several days of hard fighting, Stapp's unit was sent to the Belgium city of Liege for some rest. While there, a number of German V-1 rockets (also known as "buzz bombs") flew over, trying to cause havoc with the Allies and the civilian population. Outside of the walled city of Liege, Stapp and his unit were back in their half-tracks.

"We used those buzz bombs for target practice with our 50 caliber machine guns on the half-tracks," Stapp explained. "My troops and I shot down two of those birds."

But, the target practice came to an abrupt halt when plinking away at the V-1s caused one to go in an errant direction.

"I must have hit the stabilizer on the tail, or the gyroscope mechanism because suddenly the buzz bomb went into a slow, swooping turn, circling like a big buzzard," Stapp recalled. "Finally, it hit just on the edge of the town, missing all of my platoon. We never shot at those damned things after that."

While resting up in Liege, one of the coldest winters in the history of Europe was engulfing Belgium and western Europe. One day an officer in a Jeep pulled up alongside Sergeant Stapp and directed him and the other four halftracks to follow him. The drove to the small town of Stavelot, Belgium. They didn't know it at the time, but they were entering what would be later known in history as "The Battle of the Bulge."

The platoon of five halftracks had been temporarily assigned to Gen. George S. Patton's Third Army to help throw back the German offensive.

Stapp and his five halftracks drove through Stavelot and crossed a river at the edge of town, parking on a steep hill on the other side overlooking the village.

"Despite the brutal cold weather, my outfit made out better than the ground-pounders (infantrymen) because part of our uniform as halftrack crewmembers were heavily-padded jackets and pants," Stapp explained. "We had C-rations, which was canned meat, vegetables, and other assorted so-called 'complete meals,'" Stapp recalled. "We always had hot food when we had C-rations because I devised a holder under the hood of my halftrack where we kept the cans. The heat from the engine kept dinner simmering for whenever we had the chance to stop and eat."

As the sun set that evening, the platoon tried to make themselves comfortable as they waited for the Germans.

"About 2 o'clock in the morning I heard a scraping sound," Stapp recalled. "It sounded as though something was scraping the roadway. I took a stroll through the trees and up the hill to see what it might be."

As Stapp neared the crest of the hill, he saw a U.S. Army Jeep, but something was wrong. Then he froze in his tracks. There were three German helmets with enemy heads wearing them, sitting in the vehicle.

"I got back down to my men as quickly as possible and passed the word to the other four halftracks," Stapp recalled. "They're here!"

Just then, a lot of yelling and screaming came from up the hill and in the trees.

"I could hear the Germans alerting each other, so we immediately began firing into the trees," he said. "One out of every four of our 50 caliber bullets was an incendiary shell."

During World War II, the .50 caliber machine gun probably was the most-feared weapon on each side.

"You couldn't hide behind a tree because a .50 caliber bullet would either go right through it or cut the damned thing down," Stapp reckoned.

As the five halftrack crews fired into the trees, Stapp said he could hear a lot of screaming, moaning and groaning.

"I had one of my men fire a bazooka shell (hand-held rocket launcher) up toward the trees," he recalled.

In the heat of the battle, the American division encamped on the other side of the river in Stavelot fired a red flare, recalling the five halftracks. Stapp and his platoon didn't know it at the time, but they were directly in front of a German SS Panzer (tank) Division. When they got back across the river and into the village, they realized the "American" troops that had recalled them were actually Germans dressed in U.S. uniforms.

"They had directed us into a trap," Stapp said. "What they didn't count on was my platoon crossing the river."

As the five halftracks flew down the side of the hill toward the river, the lead halftrack was taken out by cables the Germans had stretched across the road. The cables had tangled into the vehicle's steering and front wheels, causing the driver to lose control. The halftrack slammed into the side of the hill. Stapp and his crew stopped and loaded the crashed crewmembers into their vehicle and continued down the hill.

As the platoon barreled across the bridge and into the town, there were Germans firing from both sides of the street, catching the Americans in a crossfire.

"We flew through town at what seemed like a high-rate of speed, firing in all directions while we drove," Stapp recalled. "John Wayne couldn't have had a more exciting escape scene." During the platoon's dash for freedom, another halftrack was lost. When they got to the other side of Stavelot, only one of their halftracks was left.

"Our company had gone on without us, so we were more or less stranded for eight days," Stapp said. "Of the 55 men in my platoon, only 28 of us were left."

The Battle of the Bulge was lost by the Germans primarily because they simply ran out of gas. Near where Stapp's platoon was located, the Germans made a fatal decision to follow the river instead of going up to the top of a nearby hill. Had they taken the hill, they would have found a U.S. Army fuel dump, which was totally undefended. This would have given them the precious gasoline they needed to keep their tanks rolling.

"I'll never forget the sheer exhaustion my unit and I experienced during those hectic 10 days between Dec. 16 and Dec. 26, 1944," Stapp recalled. "To me, the Battle of the Bulge meant 10 sleepless nights. I was the senior man in our unit and I had two men to a foxhole spotted strategically around in defensive positions."

'Son, Salute When You Speak to Me!'

ONE OF OCEANSIDE MORE COLORFUL and fascinating characters was the late Benjamin A. Records. Well, for sure, he was a character.

Born March 6, 1924, Benny grew up with a twin brother in Riverside. To think there were two like Ben boggles the mind.

Ben was 18 when he joined the U.S. Army Air Corps in 1942 to become a radioman. This point is important because instead of "flying" into Normandy during the June 6, 1944 D-day invasion, Benny and three other Air Corps lads landed with the very first wave of infantry troops onto Omaha Beach. Their job was to set up a communications post to direct Allied aircraft on bombing targets.

It must have been a harrowing experience wading ashore with all that radio equipment while being fired upon in one of the worst combat zones in the history of warfare.

"Naw," Ben recalled. "The four of us had .45's (pistols)."

Ben's team made it safely ashore. Many weeks later, after his unit had moved a number of times, more Air Corps personnel were brought in, including a major general (two-star).

"One night two or three of us stole the general's jeep, went into a French town and got drunk," Ben admitted. "Somehow he found out about it and was gonna pull an inspection the next morning."

Later, Ben and his buddies drove the jeep outside of the camp, disassembled it, and buried the jeep in a farmer's pasture.

"That general nearly went nuts trying to find his jeep," Ben laughed. "Some French farmer probably had himself a nice Jeep after the war."

Later, when the Allies were crossing the Rhine River into Germany, Ben's communication command was encamped on the French side while U.S. Naval personnel, using flat-bottom landing craft, were shuttling personnel and equipment across into Germany.

"The guys in my unit never wore our ranks or stripes in combat zones," Ben recalled. "I was a private, so I didn't have anything to wear, anyway."

One evening a young U.S. Navy ensign, with his gold bar quite visible, came up and asked Ben where the officer's quarters were?

Ben chuckled, then casually told him there were "a few foxholes dug along the riverbank" and the officer was welcome to one.

"Soldier, don't you believe in saluting an officer?" the ensign barked back at Ben.

Just then, Ben's commanding officer, an Army Air Corps colonel, walked up.

"Son, you'd better be careful," the colonel told the ensign. "You're addressing General Records, our commanding officer."

The young Navy ensign snapped to attention, smartly saluted Ben, then did an about face and proceeded down the riverbank to find a foxhole for the night.

When Ben returned home after the War, he became a Riverside County Sheriff's deputy, among other things, before retiring to Oceanside. He died in 2005 after a short illness.

A 'Balancing Act' to End a War

Lt. Col. Clarence Baer, USAFR-retired, had one of the most interesting and intriguing tasks to contribute greatly to the World War II effort … and he never left state-side.

WHEN I ASKED OCEANSIDE'S CLARENCE Baer what he did for Uncle Sam during the great World War II, he replied with a smile, "I served in the United States Army 'Chair' Corps."

Although he never heard a shot fired in anger, Baer had a key role in ending the war, even though at the time he didn't know he was doing it.

Baer was commissioned a 2nd lieutenant in the U.S. Army Reserve out of ROTC from Clemson University when he graduated in 1933. Born in 1911, Baer grew up in Spartansburg, S.C. He received a mechanical engineering degree. After graduation, Baer took a job with the Federal Power Commission in Washington, D.C. After a year or so, Baer was transferred to an FPC regional office in Denver.

While in Denver, Baer met and later married Louise Gregg.

"We met in the middle of a blizzard," Baer recalled. "I remember it well. It was 1937 and we were attending a ski club meeting."

Clarence and Louise married the following May in 1938. By 1939, war clouds were on the horizon and all of the aircraft companies were hiring as many engineers as they could find.

"We had a small child, but in 1939, Louise agreed with me that we should move on to California," he said. "We moved to Burbank where I went to work for Lockheed as a weight engineer."

Later that year, an Army Air Corps colonel from Wright Army Air Field in Dayton, Ohio was taking delivery of a new Lockheed C-60 plane, (forerunner of the Constellation). They got into a conversation about the looming war.

"He told me he had a job for me at Wright Field, if I wanted it, as a weights and balance officer," Baer recalled. "I figured it was a good opportunity to get in on the ground floor, so to speak, so I told him I'd go if he could get me orders."

Within a month Baer was a 1st lieutenant, stationed at the U.S. Army Air Corps Aircraft Laboratory at Wright Field near Dayton.

"I spent the next few years at Wright, never going anywhere else," he chuckled. "I was doing the same work I had been doing at Lockheed."

When he arrived at Wright Field, Baer was assigned to the Weight Branch, headed by a major who didn't know anything about weighting an aircraft. During a trip to a Pennsylvania aircraft plant, Baer not only solved a problem of proper weight and balance of aircraft being manufactured, his boss watched Baer as he did the job.

While Baer's work in the Army Air Corps didn't seem that exciting, it had its moments. Basically, it was his job to calculate and design heavy loads for planes, especially bombers, so they could get off the ground safely and fly properly.

By 1943, Baer was a captain and considered one of the Air Corps' top weight and balance experts.

One day in mid-1945, Captain Baer was told to report to a Wright Field hangar where two B-29 "Super Fortress" bombers awaited him. He knew these weren't just any bombers, but no one was saying why they were special.

"All I was told was that 'here are two aircraft that each has to be modified to carry a 'very heavy object,'" Baer recalled. "I was told what I was working on was 'more than top-secret.' It was the most important job I would ever have."

The two B-29 bombers took their turn on the huge scales in the Wright Field hangar. Baer's job was to tell other engineers where in the fuselage to place the bomb rack. The first bomber would have to be fitted for a 10,000-pound "object;" the second one, a 9,000-pound payload.

Baer said no B-29, which was the biggest bomber during the war, had ever carried a bomb load of that much weight.

"It didn't take very long for me to do the work, maybe a few weeks, and then one night the two B-29s disappeared," he chuckled. "We didn't have computers back then. I had to work out everything on a mechanical calculator and a slide ruler."

It wouldn't be until some three months after the war ended that Baer figured out he had designed the bomb loads for the "Enola Gay" and "Bock's Car," the two planes that carried the atomic bombs dropped on Japan. The Enola Gay carried "Little Boy," the 9,000-pounder; Bock's Car (named for its pilot, Fredrick C. Bock) carried "Fat Man," a 10,000-pound device.

Army Air Corps Col. Paul Tibbett, the pilot of the Enola Gay (named for his mother), said the following about the tremendous weight of "Little Boy" as it was dropped over Hiroshima:

"We were carrying such weight that when the bomb was released, the Enola Gay shot up so fast that my pilot's seat hit my ass with such tremendous force, I thought I was going to be thrown through the top of the plane."

After the war, Baer returned to civilian life and to Los Angeles. He spent 16 years working for the Northrup Corporation, where almost on his first day he saved his new employer a lot of money.

"It was left to me to explain to Jack Northrup that the new F-89 jet fighter we were building would have to be modified because someone had calculated the weight of the fuel as gasoline instead of jet fuel, which is heavier," Baer explained.

"The plane had to be redesigned for bigger tanks in order to meet the Air Corps' range specifications."

Baer joined Hughes Aircraft in 1962 where he spent another 12 years before retiring in 1974. He stayed in the U.S. Air Force Reserve, retiring as a lieutenant colonel.

For the last several years of his life, Baer spoke at high school veterans' programs, telling of his experiences during World War II.

During one such program, a young high school student raised her hand and asked, "Don't you feel guilty having played a role in the deaths of all those innocent people at Hiroshima?"

Baer shook his head and replied, "No. I actually feel good about it because I helped save a lot of lives -- including Japanese lives. Those bombs brought a quick end to the war," he concluded.

A Character Most Unforgettable

THERE WILL BE DOZENS OF reasons to go and listen to local living legends of World War II tell their stories at an annual Veterans Day Conference some years ago at El Camino High School, but one of the best was Navy Cross holder Fred Swearingen of Carlsbad. If anyone in San Diego County deserved to be on the "Most Unforgettable Character" list, Fred had all of the qualifications. In addition to holding the Navy's highest battle honor, Fred had four Distinguished Flying Crosses, and four Air Medals.

"You got an Air Medal for every five times you flew against the enemy," Fred chuckled. "I guess the Navy figured if you survived that many flights, you deserved it. Hell, if you got to meals on time, the Navy recommended you for a medal."

During the war, Fred was stationed aboard Vice Admiral Marc Mitscher's flagship, the USS Bunker Hill. Fred was trained as a dive bomber pilot at North Island Naval Air Station and, because of the war time shortage of accommodations, he was berthed at the nearby historic Hotel del Coronado.

"The first plane I flew in combat was the SB Douglas 'Dauntless' dive bomber," he said with great affection. "Then they moved us into the SB2-C Curtiss-Wright 'Helldiver,' which was much bigger, heavier and harder to fly. We called it the 'Son-of-a-Bitch-Second-Class.'"

"When not flying, pilots would gather in the ready room and play cards. If there was an attack, we'd just keep right on playing, but when those .20 millimeter shipboard guns starting firing, we'd usually stop because that meant the enemy was getting damned close."

Fred recalled one day when the Officer of the Day came in the ready room for some pilots to move 10 planes forward on the flight deck so that an incoming squadron could land.

"We (pilots) hated that detail. Plane handlers could push a plane backwards, but with wings folded and fully loaded, a dive bomber weighed 7 tons, so we had to start the engines and move them forward," he explained. "I tried to get out of the detail by hiding behind a big high-backed chair, but I got caught and the O.O.D (Officer-of-the-Day) ordered me to go topside and move planes."

Fred said after he got up on the flight deck, a Japanese kamakazi plane came straight out of nowhere, slamming into the Bunker Hill. Everyone left in the ready room where Fred had been just 10 minutes before was killed in an exploding ball of fire. Another kamakazi hit about 20 seconds later. In all, 400 sailors were killed, with 700 to 800 wounded. The Bunker Hill would end up sinking in that attack.

Fred spend 21 years as a referee for the National Football League between 1960 and 1981. He officiated Super Bowls III and XIII, but he'll be most remembered by sports fans for making the call that became a legend in football history -- "the immaculate reception" by Steeler running back Franco Harris of the Pittsburgh against the Oakland Raiders. "Because of that call, my name is boldly written on every crapper wall in Oakland and (then) Oakland Raiders head coach John Madden still hasn't forgiven me." Fred passed on in early 2017.

A Salute by CPO Victor Mature, USCG

IN ONE OF MY DAILY columns, I had written about a portion of Interstate 5 that runs through Camp Pendleton (just north of Oceanside) being dedicated to the memory of Marine Gunnery Sgt. John Basilone, a highly decorated Marine hero of World War II.

Over the years I've written a number of stories about Hollywood screen idol Victor Mature before he died on Aug. 4, 1999, in Rancho Santa Fe. But, after his demise, yet another story emerged about these two close friends.

After Sergeant Basilone was awarded the Medal of Honor for heroism on Guadalcanal, he was sent around the United States selling war bonds with a number of celebrities, including Mature, who was at that time a chief petty officer in the U.S. Coast Guard.

Vic and Basilone became good friends, but Vic constantly worried about his buddy, fearing he had a death wish. At nearly every war bond show at which the two would appear, the Marine sergeant would get up and angrily address the audience, yelling that he shouldn't be wasting his time trying to entertain them; rather, he should be "over in the Pacific killing (the enemy)!" Mamaux says Basilone never used the word "enemy," rather the accepted short, albeit derogatory, terms of "Japs" or "Nips" for the Japanese during that era.

The Marine Corps did it's best to keep Basilone out of harm's way. When Basilone wasn't selling bonds, the Corps had him working in special services as a beach lifeguard at Camp Pendleton. But the sergeant complained enough about sitting around and wanting to go back into combat, he was issued orders to return to the fighting in the Pacific.

Mamaux says Vic nearly got in trouble because of his loud protests to the Marines for sending Basilone back into combat.

"Vic was certain Basilone had a death wish, and he shouldn't be sent back," Mamaux recalled. "Vic talked about his friend countless times over those years I knew him. He did his damnedest to save Basilone. He raised so much hell with the general responsible, that Vic almost got a court martial over it."

In February 1945, Basilone landed on Iwo Jima, charged and captured a Japanese bunker single-handedly, but soon after was killed by a mortar round. He received the Silver Star posthumously.

"Every time Vic passed by Basilone Road (on Camp Pendleton), he would salute," Mamaux recalled.

Germany's 'Great Escape' Artist

You could call Oceanside's Adalbert "Bert" Messerschmitt "a great escape artist of World War II." He did it several times beginning with the Russian Front back in 1941.

Born in 1921 in the mountain resort village of Reiterswiesen, Germany in northern Bavaria, Messerschmitt was the son of a Bavarian forester. In 1937, whehe turned 17, he had to serve a year of national service, constructing the massive Siegfried Line of concrete bunkers along the western German border. When Germany invaded Poland in 1939, Messerschmitt found himself drafted into the Wehrmacht (German armed forces).

You might be wondering about that name, *Messerschmitt*. Yes, he was related.

Adalbert Messerschmitt was the grand-nephew of famed German aircraft designer and builder, Willy Messerschmitt, although he never soared to the heights of his more famous uncle. Willy Messerschmitt designed the core inventory of the German Luftwaffe, including the ME-109 fighter and later the world's first operational fighter jet, the ME-262.

"I didn't know it at the time, but in December 1941, Uncle Willy arranged to have me pulled out of the fighting in the Ukraine and sent to fighter pilot school. When I found out, it made me mad and I got a transfer back to my old army unit," he said.

The Russian campaign resulted in two memorable experiences in Messerschmitt's young life.

The first was his involvement with a Chechnyan family, in particular, a girl named Vera.

"The Chechnyans hated the Russians (as they apparently still do), so they were pretty friendly to us Germans," he explained.

Later, Messerschmitt was wounded during a battle in the Caucasus Mountains in the south of Chechnya, and, simultaneously, came down with malaria.

What happened next is somewhere between a miracle and the *"Twilight Zone."*

"I was transported back away from the fighting in a truck," he recalled. "I remember being dropped off at this fork in the road because the truck had to go another direction. Next thing I know, I'm waking up in a familiar house."

He was in the home of Vera and her Chechnan family who had befriended him earlier.

"Vera told me I had been brought to a nearby village and when word spread that a wounded German soldier was there, curiosity brought her to see if it was me," he chuckled.

While he was convalescing, a Russian scout plane flew low one evening over the village.

"We all took cover, except for Vera," he recalled. "She just laughed and told me it was her brother, a reconnaissance pilot for the Russians. He flew over the village each night to check on his family.

Messerschmitt's malaria got worse and he fell into a coma.

"I had told Vera I needed to get to a German hospital some several hundred miles to the north in Rostov," Messerschmitt recalled. "When I woke up several days later, I was at that very hospital."

When he questioned the orderlies about how he got there, they told him they didn't know, only that he was found wandering around on the road near the hospital.

"I can never prove it, but I figured that Vera's brother flew me there in his Russian scout plane, landed on the road and dropped me off," he laughed. "It's a wild, crazy story, but there it is -there's no other way it could have happened."

When he recovered, Messerschmitt was sent back to the fighting and soon found himself a prisoner of war near Uman, Ukraine.

His captivity was short-lived.

"I was with about 18 or 20 other German soldiers who were being kept by the Russians to shuttle ammunition from a supply point to their lines," he recalled.

On the third day, a German Stuka dive bomber began strafing his work column and the two Russian guards dived for cover.

Messerschmitt ran down a drainage ditch for a mile or so and buried himself into a culvert leading under a road. He packed mud to cover the opening and laid hidden until it was dark.

"At that time, it was a policy that if you were captured by the enemy and managed to escape and return, the army would transfer you out of the area," Messerschmitt explained. "As a reward, I was sent to the south of France where I was promoted to sergeant."

From 1942 to 1944 he was stationed in the south of France. On Oct. 21, 1944, he was again captured, this time by a unit of the 313th Infantry Division of the U.S. 7th Army. He remained a POW under American control until Feb. 15, 1946.

"The Americans said we could go home," Messerschmitt said. "But, something happened that wasn't supposed to. One day we were marched out of the camp and across the road to a French POW camp near Dijon, France."

Messerschmitt said he spent the next several months as a French POW. While in the French POW camp, he was put in charge of a work gang, which worked in the forest cutting firewood. After nearly two years of continued imprisonment, he'd had enough.

"The war had been over for more than a year," Messerschmitt said. "I just wanted to go home."

It was July 15, 1946, Bastille Day, a French national holiday. He knew the French guards would be celebrating and if he were going to escape, the holiday was the time to do it. It worked. Messerschmitt and three other German soldiers slipped through the barbed wire fencing and escaped into the nearby forest. Knowing the French would look directly east where the Rhine River separated France from Germany, the quartet traveled north for 13 nights when they eventually crossed the German border.

Although he was back home on German soil, his days as an escape artist weren't at an end. He and a fellow POW had managed to get into civilian clothes along with forged documents. Each village they came to required strict I.D. checks, so Messerschmitt and his POW colleagues split up and tried to avoid any uniform.

When he and a fellow POW were within a few miles of Bad Kissingen, Messerschmitt's hometown in Bavaria, they nearly were caught again, this time in a train station.

There they were, two POWs escaped from the French, sitting having a beer at this long table in the station's waiting room. Just as the train was approaching, two American MPs walked in and began checking everyone's papers. One of the young girls sitting next to Messerschmitt saw they were getting nervous and asked what was wrong.

"When I told them we were escaped POWs, she told us to slip under the table and hide under their skirts," Messerschmitt laughed. "And, that's what we did. The MPs never saw us."

He was home within an hour. It was his last escape.

In 1948, Messerschmitt met and married his wife, Rita, and worked as an apprentice with an upholsterer, then later joined the U.S. Army. He was made a master sergeant in charge of a company of German guards protecting ammo dumps, housing developments and gasoline facilities on U.S. Army bases.

With the sponsorship of his wife's aunt in Columbus, Ohio, in 1953, the Messerschmitts immigrated to the United States.

"The first thing I did when we arrived in New York City was have a banana split in a drug store," he laughed. "I'd never had one before." It was the beginning of a sweet American life.

In 1960, the couple moved to Los Angeles where Messerschmitt worked for Exact Weight Scale Co. He eventually was promoted to regional manager. In 1981, he started his own packaging company and in 1994, retired and bought a home next door to his brother, Hans, in Oceanside. "During the war, I was a loyal German soldier, but since coming to America, I'm every bit as much American as anyone born in this country, and I'm very proud of it!"

The Deadly Skies Over Europe

1st Lt Bill Ryherd, pilot of a B-26 bomber, was shot down over southern France. He was captured and sent =to a prison camp, but it's where he was sent that tells the real story.

ONE HAUNTING THOUGHT THAT WOULD never leave the upper-most mind of any crewmember of an Allied plane flying over enemy territory was having to evade and escape in case they were shot down. And, thousands of Allied fliers found themselves in such a predicament -- on the ground, scurrying for a hiding place. Some successfully made it back to friendly territory; many others were captured or, worse, killed.

The dilemma facing downed fliers was: do I stay in uniform and try to get back to safety? Or, do I get into civilian clothes and blend into the society while making good my escape? The answer was easy, but getting into civilian clothes took them out of the security of the Geneva Convention rules, and into the category of being a suspected spy. Here is the harrowing example of what happened to one such downed flier who shed his uniform to mask his identity.

Thousands of Allied fliers were forced to bail out of their crippled aircraft, or crash-landed after being hit by enemy fire while flying on bombing missions over Europe. Those not immediately captured by the Germans attempted to get back to friendly territory by evading the enemy often with the help of friendly resistance fighters, primarily in France, Belgium and Holland. When fliers would be caught wearing civilian clothes they could be treated like spies. Most were ultimately identified as Allied prisoners of war and placed in POW camps. A few, however, weren't so lucky. One of the most dramatic stories comes as a result of 162 known Allied fliers who ended up in Buchenwald Concentration Camp.

William H. "Bill" Ryherd of Oceanside spent three months in a hell on earth in late 1944, when he was held as a prisoner in Nazi Germany's infamous Buchenwald death camp.

Ryherd found himself inside of one of Hitler's concentration camps not because of religious or political beliefs, but because he was caught by the Gestapo in Paris while out of his U.S. Army Air Corps uniform trying to escape to Spain. According to Geneva Convention rules, POW status isn't required if the uniform isn't worn. As far as the Germans were concerned, he was just another civilian working against the Third Reich.

Ryherd, a native of Donna, Tex., was a first lieutenant assigned to the U.S. 9th Air Force flying a B-26 out of England. He was shot down on his 36th mission on Aug. 4, 1944. Ryherd was supposed to have taken a 10-day leave in Scotland after his 35th mission with the 397th Bombing Group, in the 598th Bombing Squadron flying out of Rivenhall, England, but he wanted to be part of a new type of bombing system called "A-zone."

A-zone was the first radio-directed bombs used in the war. The new device required the pilot fly a steady course while the bombardier guided the bombs to their target. It turned out to be a fatal move. The target was a bridge over the Seine River a few miles south of Paris. Two bursts of enemy flak ripped through Ryherd's wing tank, causing a fire. As long as fuel was leaking and the fire burning, Ryherd knew he was okay. It was when the tank was drained that vapors would explode. He had to act fast.

"I had my crew bail out," Ryherd recalled. "I tried to stay with it as long as I could, but soon after they were out, I got out of there myself."

Ryherd dropped out of his plane through the bomb bay doors at 12,000 feet using a chest parachute, which wouldn't open.

"I literally tore it (parachute) open with my hands," he recalled. "About that time my plane blew up. I got out just in time."

Ryherd landed in an open French farmer's field where workers were tilling the soil.

"I grabbed my 'chute and ran about 100 yards into the woods," he said. "I didn't know it at the time, but I had broken my ankle when I landed."

A French resistance fighter happened to be one of the workers in the field. Neither spoke the other's language, but the Frenchmen made himself understood by pointing to his watch. The farm worker would come back at midnight for the American airman.

"This guy scooped up my 'chute and took off," Ryherd chuckled. "I didn't know whether he'd bring back help or the Germans."

About midnight, the Frenchman returned with a comrade. Both were armed with automatic weapons. Ryherd went to get up out of his hiding place, discovering for the first time he had a broken ankle.

The trio traveled into a small village where a college professor hid Ryherd during the next few days. As relieved as Ryherd was that he was in the hands of the French resistance, he became nervous when the man who found him explained that "about 30 percent of the resistance fighters were loyal to France; about 30 percent to the Germans; and another 40 percent would play both sides of the fence, depending upon circumstances.

After several days of rest, the French moved Ryherd to another house where he found his co-pilot. From there, the French resistance fighters said it was possible to escape back to Allied lines from Paris by going west through the Pyrenees Mountains and into Spain. They drove into the French capital, which was still in German control. By this time, the two Americans had changed into civilian clothing.

"When we arrived in Paris, we could hear (General George) Patton's big guns to the north of the city," Ryherd said.

The resistance placed the two Yanks at a house in Paris where there was another Allied flier, a downed RAF pilot. The plan was to disguise all three fliers as part of a work gang of Frenchmen. Once outside of the city, they'd make there way to the Pyrenees Mountains and cross over into Spain and freedom.

"On the day we were to leave, came a knock on the door -- one with the right code, only it came about an hour early," Ryherd recalled. "It was one of the Frenchmen resistance guys we'd met in Paris. We went downstairs and my co-pilot and the British fliers were waiting in the car. We headed out of Paris in the right direction (south), but suddenly the driver swerved with a hard turn and we drove right in Gestapo headquarters."

Ryherd and his comrades were betrayed by a French resistance fighter called "Captain Jacque." This wouldn't be the first time Jacque would betray Allied fliers. After the war, he would be tried as a war criminal and hung. But, on this day in 1944, he would be responsible for sending Ryherd to hell on earth.

Ryherd couldn't believe the betrayal by the Frenchman, but he remembered the caution another Frenchman had given him a few days before. It was true.

"When we arrived at Gestapo Headquarters, there were German soldiers everywhere burning documents and scurrying around," Ryherd said. "They knew Patton was coming and they were trying to get out of our town."

Ryherd was surprised their interrogation was so quick and even somewhat sloppy. The airmen confessed to being Allied fliers, but the Gestapo interrogator pointed out they were in civilian clothes, no dog tags, so they must be civilians. The trio was taken to a prison where some 3,000 French men and women were being held.

It is ironic that Allied military politics prevented Ryherd and his comrades from being rescued by General Patton.

"Ike (General Dwight D. Eisenhower) made Patton halt outside of Paris until General (Charles) DeGaulle could get into position to lead the Allied troops into the city," Ryherd said. "This delay gave the Germans a chance to ship all of us in that prison out of town on railroad cars."

The next five days were a precursor to what lie ahead. Among the 2,000 men and 1,000 women jammed 95-plus into railroad cars designed to hold only 40 people, were some 162 Allied fliers including Ryherd and his two comrades.

"An ol' boy from Texas told me as we were heading east toward Germany and that we were being taken to a concentration camp," Ryherd said. "I told him he was wrong, that the Germans knew who we were and we'd surely be taken off the train in Frankfurt. Boy was I wrong."

With more than 95 souls jammed into Ryherd's car, there was not enough room to do anything but stand. The train stopped from time-to-time for toilet breaks, off-loading, and re-loading the prisoners. About the second day out, Ryherd noticed a line forming in his car. He didn't know what it was for, but figured it might be food, so he wanted his share.

"One of the Frenchmen found a loose board in the railroad car," Ryherd recalled. "It was just big enough to drop one person at a time out onto the track, so if you lie prone until the train passed, you could get up and started running."

There was just one problem with that thinking. No one knew if there was an engine "pusher" at the rear of the train. If that be the case, the cowcatcher on the front of the second locomotive would grind up anyone laying on the tracks.

"I was number 9, ready to go and take my chances," Ryherd said. "The guy ahead of me chickened out and refused to go, causing such a commotion the German guards in the next car heard us."

Seven prisoners made good their escape. One was a U.S. flier, a friend of Ryherd's. He learned later there was no "pusher" at the end of the train. "I found out later that guy made it back to England," he recalled.

The Germans were furious at losing the seven Allied prisoners. One of the guards announced that for every escapee, five would be shot the next day. Sure enough, the next day the train stopped in a country clearing, the doors were opened on Ryherd's car and one of the guards shouted "35 of you get out!"

Ryherd was near the entrance of the car and was forced out with the other 34.

"I can tell you there were no atheists among us on that day," he chuckled. "Everyone, except one, was saying their prayers. And the one who wasn't was reading his New Testament."

Just then a group of German officers walked up to inquire what was going on. After a quick huddle, the guards ordered the 35 back into the rail car.

"You never saw 35 people move that fast," he said.

Earlier, the 35, including Ryherd, had been ordered to take off every stitch of clothing. Even though it was August and hot during the day, the nights were quite cold, he recalled. The 35 huddled together trying to draw warmth from each other.

While stopped in a town just past the German border, a shot rang out. One of the guards had fired into Ryherd's car. The shot had hit one of the prisoners in the hand. It wasn't clear whether he was a Frenchman or Allied flier, but the Germans took him off the train and shot him in the back of the head and twice in the chest.

"They (Germans) were proving to us they meant business," Ryherd said. "When we got to Frankfurt, they gave us back our clothes."

After five days of standing in the cramped rail cars, the train arrived at Buchenwald Concentration Camp with the 3,000 some prisoners on Aug 21, 1944. Buchenwald is located south and east of Berlin about 50 miles. It was one of the earliest of death camps established by Hitler.

"The first thing the Germans did when we arrived was group us into five columns at 10 people deep," Ryherd recalled. "Next, we were herded over to an area where Russian prisoners of war were shaving every hair on every new prisoner's body, head-to-toe. From there we walked down into a cattle dip-affair for delousing."

(The Soviet Union was not a signer of the Geneva Convention, hence Russian military personnel, when captured, was treated differently than other Allied POWs by being place in the death camps).

The prisoners were given khaki jackets and pants, but no cap and no shoes.

Because the concentration camp was not designed for prisoners of war, it was built adjacent to a German ammunition factory, a big target which the Royal Air Force frequently found on its nightly bombing raids.

"We were called out frequently to fight fires after the bombing, and we were barefoot," Ryherd said. "One of our guys made some shoes from a couple of pieces of wood, but a German guard saw him and nearly beat him to death with a large wooden stick."

A few days after they arrived in Buchenwald, the 162 Allied fliers were moved into a large barracks were some 250 or more young gypsy children aged 8 to 13 years were being kept.

"They were mean little guys," Ryherd recalled. "They'd steal anything worth stealing, just to survive."

Ryherd learned later the Germans loaded the children onto two railroad car where they were gassed.

"I saw that myself," he said. "I later learned one little guy escaped and ended up being educated in this country."

Ryherd said the organization of the camp was fascinating. The German military guards were around the perimeter of the compound, but German civilian prisoners (not Jews) actually ran the camp inside. Jews were being gassed by day while the crematorium furnaces raged at night. But, not everyone who was murdered was gassed. A group of British Secret Service agents, who had been captured behind enemy lines working with the French, were ceremoniously hung in front of all the prisoners during the evening roll call. The Geneva Convention rules didn't apply to them either. "The German civilians running the inside of the camp realized who we were and kept us Americans out of going on the work details," he recalled.

How the 162 prisoners got out of the death camp isn't quite clear, but one of the most commonly told stories has a Russian prisoner on a work detail informing the Luftwaffe (German Air Force) commandant at a nearby airfield about the Allied fliers who were being held at Buchenwald. The Luftwaffe commandant reportedly went to the camp and demanded the flier be turned over to him. When the S.S. commandant refused, the Luftwaffe commandant informed the other than he was a personal friend of Reichmarshal Hermann Goering and that the second-ranked Nazi behind Hitler would not want Allied prisoners mistreated. The next day, all but one of the Allied fliers were turned over to the Luftwaffe and headed for Stalag Luft III. The flier left behind was in the camp hospital and reportedly died.

"Word on the grapevine was that we were less than 24-hours from being executed," Ryherd said. "When we were interviewed by the S.S. right before our release from Buchenwald, we thought that was it. The next day, (Oct. 21, 1944), we were loaded onto trucks and taken to a train station."

Stalag Luft III was where the famous "Great Escape" was attempted earlier that same year. Ryherd was housed in the RAF section of the compound on the north side.

Although they didn't know each other, there were two downed Allied fliers who eventually ended up living in North San Diego County, California. They both were on forced march in the bitter winter cold from Luft III to Nuremberg in January 1945. One of them was Ryherd, the other was John "Jack" Kellogg of Vista, both no longer with us.

2nd Lt. Jack Kellogg, a co-pilot, had been shot down and captured during a B-17 bombing run out of Italy over Hungary.

After several weeks in Nuremberg, a city under constant Allied bombing attacks, the Allied POWs were moved on to Mooseburg near Munich in southern Germany. It was in Mooseburg that General Patton's Third Army finally caught up with Ryherd and Kellogg for their rescue.

"When I saw him (Patton) come riding up in his Jeep through the front gate, I thought he was the second coming. … Jesus Christ himself," Ryherd laughed. "He (Patton) gave a short speech and even apologized for being late."

After the War, Ryherd spent more than 30 years as an oil company executive in California. As he told his story, his wife and daughter listened intently from another room. Afterward, they got me aside and said it was the first time they knew anything about what Bill had gone through.

U.S. Army Air Corps pilot William "Bill" Ryherd as he appeared a few years prior to his death in 2012.

Max: Portrait of a Small-Town American

(left): U.S. Army Air Corps flying cadet Max Morrow in his flight training uniform in Santa Ana, California.
(Right) 2nd Lt. Max Morrow with his new bride, Maxine.

HE WAS TYPICAL OF THE millions of Midwestern boys from small town America, who answered the call to duty. Max Raymond Morrow grew up during the Great Depression in a home where there always was plenty to eat, but money hardly existed. His father was a butcher serving area farmers, who paid for his services primarily via barter. It was common place to sell a pound of hamburger for a dozen eggs or a gallon of milk or cream.

He was a standout high school football player as an end. He graduated in 1936 at the age of 16, but had to wait until he turned 17 before he could get a job in the International Harvester "Farmall" factory in Moline, Ill.

Max worked at Farmall until 1938, then returned home to go into the meat market and processing business with his father. Max had a new idea how to improve business: add a cold-storage locker section to the retail meat market that would allow customers to bring their foodstuffs to preserve – this was at a time when home freezers were something for the distant future.

In 1940, however, his plans were halted. With the World War looming, in 1940, Max was the first young man to be drafted from his home county.

His draft obligation was for one year. He was assigned to a coastal artillery unit on Point Loma overlooking San Diego Bay. Pearl Harbor was weeks away, but it was apparent there would be more than a year obligation was on the horizon. So when the Army Air Corps put out a call for pilot training, Max signed up and soon found himself 60 miles north in Santa Ana for basic aviation training.

As his training progressed, he found himself learning to fly a Stearman trainer in San Antonio, Texas, then on to multi-engine training in Wendover, Utah. The Boeing B-17 Flying Fortress became his designated plane. It was the biggest plane in the U.S. arsenal. It was a 10-man crew ship. As big as it was, Max laughed as he talked about his first "solo" flight.

"I was taking my final check with a training pilot. We were doing "touch and go" landings, going around the field," he recalled. "On the last go around, the trainer indicated I should taxi over to the tower. I started to shut down the engine, but the trainer told me not to."

Max chuckled. "He told me to 'take her around.'"

After several more weeks of training, Max qualified as a plane commander. He would be the pilot in charge of the plane and crew. Later, Max was on his way with a temporary skeleton crew to Washington State to receive a new B-17 at the Boeing factory in Moses Lake. He then flew to Wendover for more training with his new plane.

Next stop for Max and his new B-17 to fly to Grand Island, Neb., where a permanent crew would be assembled and assigned to him and his plane. Max wanted to name his plane "Maxine" after his new bride and high school sweetheart, but the crew voted the moniker of "Daylight Knight."

From Grand Island the new crew and plane flew to Bangor, Maine where they joined up with a dozen or so other B-17s making ready to cross the North Atlantic. The group took off early one morning and flew in formation until bad weather forced them down at Nutts Corner near Belfast, Northern Ireland. They landed in a downpour. The wing commander of the group said everyone was restricted to the base as they would be leaving for England the next day.

It was January 1944. The group landed, spread out over several English airfields.

When asked where he was based in England, Max chuckled, "I don't know, I never got off base."

But, how did you know where to land?

"I just followed the plane ahead of me."

Max wasn't in England long enough to visit any of the nearby villages or cities. As near can be determined by locating his squadron and unit, the 457th Bomb Group in the 1st Division of the 8th Army Air Corps, the air field was somewhere around Glatton, about 90 miles north of London.

Almost immediately after arriving in England, Max found himself flying his first mission over Germany. He and his crew returned from the bombing run safe and sound. The second scheduled mission had to be aborted because of engine problems. The third mission was another matter.

The target on that third mission was the ball bearing factories in Schweinfurt, Germany. It was one of the biggest and most important targets of the war, but it wasn't the first time over that target. Earlier, hundreds of planes had been launched with heavy losses. It would be the same on Feb. 24, 1944.

Earlier Schweinfurt bombing raids in October 1943, caused German factories to be badly hit, but the missions failed to achieve any lasting effect. The production of ball bearings in the factories was halted for only six weeks and Germany's war industry could easily rely on its substantial inventory of ball bearings as well as a large production surplus. In addition, the ball bearing facilities were dispersed to reduce their bombing risk. But the biggest factor in the earlier missions failure was because they were unescorted daylight raids deep into Germany. As a result, they were suspended until the February 1944's "Big Week" missions that included P51-B Mustang fighter escorts.

On that Feb. 24 flight, all went well until the "Daylight Knight" was over the target. The plane was hit by flak from the deadly .88 millimeter artillery cannons disabling engines 1 and 2. Navigator 1st Lt. Daren A. McIntyre was seriously wounded and ball-turret gunner, Sgt. Italo Stella, was killed by shrapnel piercing his flak jacket.

Max had a decision to make – try to limp back to England on two engines or crash land in the hope his navigator could get medical treatment. He chose the latter.

Max and his co-pilot, 2nd Lt. Thomas G. Davis, were able to successfully land the plane in a field and were quickly surrounded by civilians. Unfortunately, Lieutenant McIntyre did not survive. A short time later two German officers, possibly Gestapo agents, arrived and took charge. The crew soon was transported to an interrogation center.

After some time, Max and other members of the crew found themselves in Stalag I, a prisoner-of-war camp near Barth, Germany in the far northeast corner of the country on the Baltic Sea. As with all of the other German POW camps, conditions were very poor with little food. The weather was miserably cold.

Max and his crew would spend 15 months in Stalag I before being liberated by the Russian Red Army in April 1944.

When he was discharged, Max traveled to California to visit with Lieutenant McIntyre's parents, explaining how their son died. He didn't go directly back to Iowa, rather he stayed with an older brother in Lincoln, Nebraska. He didn't want to face friends and neighbors back in his hometown, who would be intent on asking a lot of questions – and, he was right. He needed time to adjust to be back in the United States and free.

Max Morrow went back to being in business with his father, where he spent the rest of his life being a success. A reporter from his hometown newspaper wrote: *"Without failure, Max slipped back into small town life."*

But, he never talked about his war experiences – never, until about 35 years later.

It all came out. He answered every question put to him. He went back to San Diego's Point Loma where he saw his old barracks building, now being used by the U.S. Navy. On a visit to San Diego's Aerospace Museum, he saw a Stearman trainer, an exact model as the one on which he learned to fly.

Being able to talk about his war experiences seem to bring a certain peace to this small-town Midwesterner member of the "Greatest Generation." Max passed away on Aug. 25, 1997 at the age of 77 well-lived years.

Editor's Note: *The stories in this book were written over a period years. Most, but not all, of the characters we've written about are no longer with us. All of the World War II men have passed on. In writing this book, we wanted to get down on paper some of the better stories of our lives before the colors fade. We did it primarily for our families, friends and former colleagues. -30-*

In our younger years the four of us writers, along with an ad guy, would get together for weekends of fun. Above, left to right: Sam Lowe, Cecil Scaglione, John Beatty, Ad guy Jim Cotton hoisting a beer and Tom Morrow.

Made in the USA
Monee, IL
05 November 2021